Cambridge Elements

Elements in Austrian Economics
edited by
Peter Boettke
George Mason University

UNDERSTANDING LUDWIG LACHMANN'S ECONOMICS

Virgil Henry Storr
George Mason University

Solomon M. Stein
George Mason University

CAMBRIDGE
UNIVERSITY PRESS

CAMBRIDGE
UNIVERSITY PRESS

Shaftesbury Road, Cambridge CB2 8EA, United Kingdom

One Liberty Plaza, 20th Floor, New York, NY 10006, USA

477 Williamstown Road, Port Melbourne, VIC 3207, Australia

314–321, 3rd Floor, Plot 3, Splendor Forum, Jasola District Centre,
New Delhi – 110025, India

103 Penang Road, #05–06/07, Visioncrest Commercial, Singapore 238467

Cambridge University Press is part of Cambridge University Press & Assessment,
a department of the University of Cambridge.

We share the University's mission to contribute to society through the pursuit of
education, learning and research at the highest international levels of excellence.

www.cambridge.org
Information on this title: www.cambridge.org/9781009479363

DOI: 10.1017/9781009083539

When citing this work, please include a reference to the DOI 10.1017/9781009083539

First published 2023

A catalogue record for this publication is available from the British Library.

ISBN 978-1-009-47936-3 Hardback
ISBN 978-1-009-08766-7 Paperback
ISSN 2399-651X (online)
ISSN 2514-3867 (print)

Cambridge University Press & Assessment has no responsibility for the persistence
or accuracy of URLs for external or third-party internet websites referred to in this
publication and does not guarantee that any content on such websites is, or will
remain, accurate or appropriate.

Understanding Ludwig Lachmann's Economics

Elements in Austrian Economics

DOI: 10.1017/9781009083539
First published online: December 2023

Virgil Henry Storr
George Mason University

Solomon M. Stein
George Mason University

Author for correspondence: Virgil Henry Storr, vstorr@gmu.edu

Abstract: Ludwig Lachmann is a central but underappreciated figure within the Austrian school of economics. Although his understanding of institutions, his appreciation of the heterogeneity of capital, his emphasis on subjectivity, and his focus on the dynamism and uncertainty of the real world have become dominant positions among Austrian economists, he is still viewed as something of an outsider. As such, the contributions of Lachmann's economics are arguably misunderstood. This Element attempts to tease out and discuss the critical contributions of Lachmann's economics. Arguably, one way in which to understand Lachmann's economics is by seeing it as unified in considering, in various ways, a single conceptual "problem" – the apparent tension between the dynamic nature of social reality and the intelligible nature of the social world. Approaching Lachmann with this theme in mind allows us to put things together more coherently than other exegetical strategies.

Keywords: Ludwig Lachmann, plan, institutions, Austrian economics, F.A. Hayek

ISBNs: 9781009479363 (HB), 9781009087667 (PB), 9781009083539 (OC)
ISSNs: 2399-651X (online), 2514-3867 (print)

Contents

1 Introduction

Ludwig Lachmann is a central but underappreciated figure within the Austrian school of economics. Although his understanding of institutions, his appreciation of the heterogeneity of capital, his emphasis on subjectivity, and his focus on the dynamism and uncertainty of the real world have become dominant positions among Austrian economists, he is still viewed as something of an outsider. Moreover, Lachmann is viewed more as a gadfly than a positive contributor to Austrian economics. As such, the contributions of Lachmann's economics are arguably misunderstood.

Unlike other key figures within Austrian economics, Lachmann's central ideas are not laid out systematically in a single volume.[1] Instead, Lachmann's economics is developed across several books. *Capital and Its Structure* (1956), building upon Hayek's ideas, sketches out an alternative to seeing capital as a homogenous aggregate and identifies some of the associated consequences for macroeconomic theory. In *The Legacy of Max Weber* (1971), Lachmann uses an assessment of Weber's methodological ideas as a jumping-off point to develop a subjectivist theory of institutions and institutional change. And, in Lachmann's *The Market as an Economic Process* (1986), he examines how characteristic differences between particular classes of markets influence the resulting exchange processes taking place within them. His essays and articles have also been collected in several edited volumes. The lectures of all three speakers at the South Royalton conference were published as *The Foundations of Modern Austrian Economics* (1976), edited by Edwin Dolan, in which Lachmann's chapters cover the market process, capital theory, and the Austrian school's critique of contemporary macroeconomics. There have also been collections of Lachmann's own writings, including the volume edited by Walter Grinder, *Capital, Expectations, and the Market Process* (1977) and *Expectations and the Meaning of Institutions* (1994), edited by Don Lavoie. As these volume titles suggest, even as Lachmann covered a wide range of topics in his writing, he returned frequently to some key themes, including capital theory and its consequences for macroeconomics, understanding economic activity in terms of processes, and the importance of subjective phenomena such as meanings and expectations. Lachmann's writing also frequently touched upon the history of economic thought and then-contemporary debates within economics as they appeared from his perspective, including a particular interest in the development of post-Keynesianism.

Others have recognized that Lachmann occupies this peculiar position within Austrian economics. Walter Grinder, in his introduction to a collection of essays by Ludwig Lachmann published in 1977, for instance, began with the observation

---

[1] See, for instance, Mises' *Human Action* (1949).

(Lachmann 1977: 3) that "for more than fifty years Ludwig M. Lachmann has been participating in scholarly debates on the development and application of economic theory; yet he is relatively unknown to professional economist and the intellectual community at large . . . Lachmann remains an outsider." Don Lavoie, writing in *his* introduction to a collection of Lachmann's essays published in 1994, similarly suggested that (Lachmann 1994: 1) "his [i.e., Lachmann's] message has not been adequately appreciated, even by those who know some of his major works. As a dissident member of a dissident school of thought, the Austrian school, his work is not well known in the economics profession at large." Storr (2019: 64), in an essay that was originally a keynote address to a conference celebrating the intellectual legacy of Ludwig Lachmann delivered in 2017 argued "that, despite the recognition he has and does receive, Lachmann does not get his due."[2]

In many ways, Lachmann's travels and professional fortunes serve as synecdoche for those of the ideas to which he was committed over that same period. Born in Germany in 1906 and entering the University of Berlin in 1924, Lachmann was, first of all, a product of the same intellectual environment of German-language academia that incubated the Austrian school as it was being developed by Carl Menger, Ludwig von Mises, and others.[3] Lachmann, however, was not initially a part of the school itself. His doctoral supervisor was Werner Sombart, leader of the German Historical School, which opposed the Austrians during the *Methodenstreit*.[4] Like so many others, the political and economic upheaval of the early 1930s saw Lachmann depart Germany, in his case, for England.

Although already having received his doctorate in Berlin, he became a student at the London School of Economics under F. A. Hayek. In 1933, then, Lachmann is in the most important academic environment in interwar economics, studying with the preeminent rising academic member of the Austrian school. This was to prove the high-water mark for the incorporation of distinctively Austrian elements into the neoclassical system. As Lachmann (1994: 160) recalls, "When I arrived at the London School of Economics in the spring of 1933, all important economists there were Hayekians. At the end of the decade Hayek was a rather lonely figure." While the 1930s were a period where Austrian ideas, particularly as developed in Hayek's work, were front-and-center of the professional and practical controversies of the day, the perception became that the distinctive positions of the Austrian school had been conclusively disproven. The decline of the Austrian school within the economics discipline was a loss that Lachmann

---

[2] See also Lewin (2018).

[3] See Dekker (2016) for an interesting exploration of the intellectual and cultural milieu that gave rise to the Austrian economics.

[4] Eicholz (2017) explores in detail Lachmann's work in Berlin and his relationship to the German Historical School in general. See also Fritz and Novak (2022).

felt particularly keenly. We can attribute this in part to his having gravitated to Austrian economics in particular due to the very elements that were now entirely out of favor.

Lachmann became all the more remote when he relocated to the University of Witwatersrand in Johannesburg in 1948. But, when the Austrian school and its ideas made their return within academic economics in the early 1970s, Lachmann, too, was able to return from his and the school's so-called "years in the wilderness" (1994: 161). Lachmann was one of the three keynote speakers for the 1974 conference at South Royalton, arguably the critical date in the revival of the Austrian school (Vaughn 1994). And, then, in the following years, we find Lachmann, as a visiting professor at New York University, once more at the epicenter of the Austrian school's intellectual activity. As Vaughn (1994: 139, fn. 2) notes in her account of the Austrian revival, "either graduate training at New York University or participation in the visiting program there virtually became a defining characteristic of a new Austrian economist in the 1980s."

This project attempts to tease out and discuss the critical contributions of Lachmann's economics. Arguably, one way in which to understand Lachmann's economics is by seeing it as unified in considering, in various ways, a single conceptual "problem" – the apparent tension between the dynamic nature of social reality and the intelligible nature of the social world. Approaching Lachmann with this theme in mind allows us to put things together more coherently in at least two ways. First, it provides a lodestar for one significant component of Lachmann's corpus, in particular his methodological contributions, history of thought essays, and works of doctrinal disputation. Indeed, centering the problem of coordination suggests an avenue for assessing what Lachmann viewed as the major achievements and open challenges for the social sciences in understanding the social world. How Lachmann understood those difficulties, however, is not purely of interest as a methodological or interpretive tool. Once we know to look at Lachmann's work from this perspective, we can identify deep interconnections among what might otherwise be seen as the disjointed topics of his contributions regarding economics "proper" (particularly his work on expectations, capital, and institutions).

One question we might ask is why a new introduction to Lachmann's ideas? One reason is that already noted: Lachmann's stock has simultaneously risen and yet remains (in our assessment) undervalued. This is not, however, simply a matter of ensuring that Lachmann is assigned "enough" importance as a member of the Austrian school from which the contemporary research program of market process theory originates, or of exhaustive "score settling" concerning the debates in which Lachmann participated – although of course where the debates concern not least the interpretation of Lachmann's arguments themselves then taking some position is unavoidable. If the goal were, after all, to make the cause for mere recognition or "correctness," we could have easily chosen a title like *Appreciating Lachmann's Influence* or *Why Lachmann's Critics Were Wrong* or similar. Instead, implicit in choosing *Understanding Ludwig Lachmann's Economics* is a slightly different aim, the provision of what we will describe later as an open-ended introduction to Lachmann's work and his ideas, a potential point of orientation both to the reading of Lachmann as a primary source and to the possible complementarities offered by engagement more directly with Lachmann's ideas for contemporary research. This approach to engaging Lachmann is endorsed by none other than Lachmann himself, as his view was that "The history of thought is a critical enterprise. Every idea contributed in the past stands in need of frequent re-examination and reinterpretation. The more important we think an idea, the more often we shall have to do that" (Lachmann 1971: ix).

The organization of the subsequent exegetical material, therefore, begins by looking at how Lachmann understood what "the difficulties inherent in mutual coordination" means and their implications, then turning to how the central areas of Lachmann's theoretical-conceptual writing come as a response to the research agenda suggested by focusing upon them. We argue that Lachmann's economics is primarily concerned with the problem of coordination. Section 2 discusses Lachmann's radical subjectivism, the consequences of active minds and the problem of kaledic nihilism. Next, Section 3, explores Lachmann's understanding markets as adjustment processes for reconciling plans, the challenge of plan adjustment outside a market, and the role of institutions. Section 4, then, explores the self-similar structure of social systems, the notion of orientation, and the centrality of the plan in Lachmann's economics. We also return to and extend our discussion of Lachmann's understanding of the concept and role of institutions. In Section 5, we discuss Lachmann's treatment of capital goods as institutions. Finally, Section 6 concludes with a discussion of Lachmann's legacy.

2 Radical Subjectivism, the Consequences of Active Minds, and the Problem of Kaledic Nihilism

The starting point for any study of Lachmann's ideas (and arguably Austrian economics) is certain to be *subjectivism*.[5] As Lachmann writes, "The first, and most prominent, feature of Austrian economics is a radical subjectivism, today no longer confined to human preferences but extended to expectations" (Lachmann 1978b: 1). Indeed, Lachmann is often accurately identified as the standard bearer

---

[5] See also Lavoie (1991) for a discussion of the centrality of subjectivism in understanding the uniqueness of the Austrian school.

of the radical subjectivist position. As Loasby (1998: 14) argued, "Lachmann was the most resolute advocate of subjectivism as the means of investigating the consequences of individual purposes, understanding and expectations, all of which differ between people, and change with time and experience." Similarly, as Vaughn (1994) described, many of the developments within the modern Austrian school can be understood as attempts to either tease out the implications of subjectivism as discussed by Lachmann or to fortify Austrian economics against Lachmann's radical subjectivism. As she (Vaughn 1994: 114) writes,

> Lachmann had initially joined Kirzner in convincing the new Austrians that their strength lay in a theory of the market process. Now he was offering suggestions on how to proceed with developing such a theory. By identifying radical subjectivism, time, and methodological individualism as the cornerstones of Austrian economics, he was in fact emphasizing those parts of Mises that were most different from mainstream economics and were also most faithful to the original Mengerian program. As it turned out, by focusing on subjectivism, time, and methodological individualism, Lachmann also was inadvertently giving the new Austrians their marching orders. Almost all subsequent writing was to be an elaboration of some implication of these themes.[6]

Subjectivism is an idea with multiple significances. It was, first, a methodological position and Lachmann's preferred covering term for the overall school of social scientific thought to which he belonged. Subjectivism in Lachmann is additionally used to express certain elements of Lachmann's ontological priors, particularly his rejection of deterministic representations of human choice. Therefore, (methodological) subjectivism is both the context in which the theoretical challenges Lachmann discusses concerning mutual coordination are raised and itself (in the "radical," ontological sense) one reason they are particularly formidable (and thus important) for him.

Methodological subjectivism, as defined by Lachmann (1994: 237), "is a research programme of the social sciences which aims at elucidating social phenomena in terms of their *inherent meaning*, i.e. in terms of their meaning to actors." We can enumerate the claims undergirding this definition, beginning from the almost trivial to the more significant:

(1) People (in the loosest sense) interact with the world in a way radically unlike the rest of the objects around them, and thus give rise to the features of events and classes of events that make up the realm of the "social."

---

[6] Here Lachmann is simply echoing Hayek (1955: 31), who famously argued that "it is probably no exaggeration to say that every important advance in economic theory during the last hundred years was a further step in the consistent application of subjectivism."

(2) The source of the distinctly "social" is individuals' possession of an autonomous internal faculty of evaluation and decision-making that stands in a causally prior relationship to their observable action, the "active mind."

(3) Social phenomena are of a qualitatively distinct character from those examined in the natural sciences because of their origination in the mental processes of the intrinsically teleological "active mind."

(4) This changes the understanding that study of social phenomena can provide into their nature vis-à-vis the physical sciences.

(5) Our ability to engage in the intelligible reconstruction of the meanings located within the unobservable domain of other individuals' active minds is possible at all because we (a) recognize those minds as mirrors of our own cognition and, on that basis, (b) identify the structural logic which gives rise to meaning.

(6) The mental object in which these various sorts of concepts and their relations are ultimately brought into coherence is "the plan," which therefore serves as the basic analytical unit of subjectivist inquiry.

Lachmann's understanding of methodological subjectivism here is firmly in line with others in the Austrian school. Recall that Mises observed that "ours is a science of meaning." As Mises (1949: 26) stated, "we cannot approach our subject if we disregard the meaning which acting man attaches to the situation, i.e., the given state of affairs, and to his behavior with regard to this situation." Similarly, Hayek has remarked that "the facts of the social sciences are what people think and believe." Also, "unless we can understand what acting people mean by their actions any attempt to explain them . . . is bound to fail" (Hayek 1955: 53). And, "it is probably no exaggeration to say that every important advance in economic theory during the last hundred years was a further step in the consistent application of subjectivism" (Hayek 1955: 31).

Lachmann, then, in focusing on the meanings that individuals attach to their actions as the way to understand human action is hardly breaking new ground. Lachmann's elucidation of the consequences of active minds and his elevation of "the plan" as being key to understanding human action were, however, quite novel. Indeed, subjectivism, as Lachmann understood it, appreciates the significance of the active mind's fundamentally autonomous and creative nature. The active mind is capable of change independent of external causal factors and therefore capable of the production of genuine novelty. Although subject to boundaries and constraints, these features of the active mind make the realm of the subjective one characterized by perpetual change of an open-ended character. It is not confined to any well-defined "range." Stated another way, while bounded, the "possible action space" is of infinite volume because of the ever-present potential for creative variations even of otherwise similar actions. Our understanding of action must therefore reflect these features of the active mind. Lachmann (2020: 55) describes this as a shift from "subjectivism as the expression of human 'disposition' to subjectivism as a manifestation of spontaneous action."

According to Lachmann, the implications of this for economic methodology are profound. It is, for instance, difficult to consider the consequences of open-endedness when employing entirely self-contained constructs like preference maps and the tools of constrained maximization. Remaining within these constructs limits the extent to which we can understand the role of creativity and interpretation. Even worse is the inherent stasis of deploying a "snapshot" when dealing with the dynamic character of the active mind. In essence, time and knowledge (or, more carefully, the elapsing of time and changes in knowledge) are consubstantial.[7] Foremost, the recognition of the significance of the active mind calls for the reaffirmation of the nondeterministic nature of social phenomena, over and against the temptation to use static devices to "understand" action as a form of mechanical response given certain (subjective) data. "The autonomy of the mind," Lachmann argues, "precludes determinism: If knowledge shapes action and action shapes the human world, the future is unpredictable" (1978b: 15).[8]

Importantly, the stronger one's commitment to the autonomous capacities of the active mind, the more serious a challenge that capacity represents to the subjectivist methodological program and its goal of understanding. Indeed, the very mental entities and their subcomponents that subjectivism identifies as the underlying cause of social phenomena could, without any outward indication *and for no reason whatsoever* (extrinsic or otherwise) alter any and all of their salient features, or simply cease to exist. As Lachmann (1971: 11) explains, "any initial situation, however much care we take to define it precisely and objectively, may suddenly … turn into another different situation merely because the individuals acting have 'changed their minds.'" Worse, this is not a mere theoretical "capacity" but one which, Lachmann (2020: 4) believes, is *ceaselessly taking place*, as "time cannot elapse without knowledge changing." The world of the mind is perpetually undergoing changes which, being

---

[7] On this, see Lachmann (1977: 90).

[8] Arguably, this was the point at which Lachmann's methodology was anchored into ontological bedrock. While in a methodological context he is willing (Lachmann 1977: 167) to defend the autonomy of the mind as a "useful hypothesis which has not hitherto been invalidated," this qualification is a lone island amid a sea of quotations whose tone is more in keeping with the one preceding it. (Even this concession, although not insincere, appears in a context where it serves more as rhetorical apophasis than anything else.)

fundamentally open-ended, can never be entirely captured in terms of a given pattern or rule.

Lachmann's ontologically subjectivist emphasis and amplification of the unbounded and incessant flux inherent to the active mind suggests the possibility that even "the plan," which Lachmann identifies as the core analytical object of interest in (methodologically) subjectivist explanation, is impermissibly static. Perversely, placing a greater emphasis upon the autonomous and open-ended nature of the active mind as part of an effort to defend its teleological weight would appear now to be ultimately fatal to the relevance of its teleological elements. The active mind's efforts to engage in goal-directed action may be hopeless in the face of the arbitrary and rapidly shifting state of the mind itself. Certainly, placing greater emphasis upon the possibility of ceaseless and unpredictable autonomous shifts in knowledge makes such a conclusion that much harder to dismiss.

This conclusion marks our first encounter with kaledic nihilism – the possibility that within a certain situation or context the disruptive effects of endogenous change are so overwhelming that no further analysis is possible. Despite what would seem to be the thrust of his emphasis on the open-endedness attributable to the active mind, Lachmann does not conclude that individual action represents a situation subject to kaledic nihilism. He does not reject kaledic nihilism, however, because he views the forces that make it appear plausible as insignificant. Instead, Lachmann believes that there are stabilizing forces at work that compensate for the very real impact of the active mind's constant activity. What those forces are, how effective they may be, and any consequences of the way in which they operate thus become basic questions of understanding social action.

In the case of the individual's action over the course of time, Lachmann (1971: 37) points out that while action is

> not determinate ... neither is it arbitrary. It is bounded, firstly, by the scarcity of means at the disposal of actors ... secondly, by the circumstance that, while men are free to choose ends to pursue, once they have made their choice they must adhere to it if consistent action with a chance of success is to be possible at all.

When we observe an acting individual, we can at least be sure that the plan to which those actions are oriented is one which that individual believes, at that time, will achieve the most desirable combination of ends with the most economy of available means. Part of the explanation of why individual action is sufficiently coherent to be an intelligible object of study is that it resides within the scaffolding of logical relationships (indeed, tautologies) following from action's teleological character, which Lachmann, following Hayek (1948: 47) at times referred to as the "Pure Logic of Choice."

The presence of such an overall structure, of course, can only really serve as a starting point to addressing the specifically *kaledic* component of the kaledic nihilism problem. The active mind could remain impossible to understand despite our knowledge of its structural logic due to the possibility that the acting individual's knowledge changes at a sufficiently rapid rate that the coherent plan at one instant gives way to a discontinuous but equally coherent plan at the next, fast enough perhaps that none of those plans are given more than trivial manifestations in action. If the only things we could know were what we could conclude on the basis of the Pure Logic of Choice, Lachmann (1977: 84) points out that it would indeed be the case that the consequence of rapid changes in knowledge and plans would be that "there could be no testing of plans, no plan revision, no comparison between *ex ante* and *ex post*. In fact, planned action would make no sense whatsoever." Lachmann, however, argues that we can understand why the "threat" of kaledic nihilism regarding individual action is not realized if instead of approaching the problem as one in which the active mind employs an undifferentiated stock of "knowledge" that is subject to endogenous change that, above a certain rate, implies a situation of kaledic nihilism, we also recognize the potential for different properties to be possessed by different types of knowledge.

Although the open-ended nature of the active mind means we can never treat these categorizations as a certainty, in general, different types of knowledge will vary in (among other characteristics) how prone they are to the sort of autonomous revisions that concern us here. As the purest expression of the essential autonomy of the individual mind, ends are likely subject to the least stability, but because those ends are pursued via drawing upon a range of other types of knowledge that have greater intertemporal coherence, we are generally able to connect actions over time. Additionally, although Lachmann understands the active mind to involve a continually changing configuration of knowledge, internal autonomous changes are unlikely to be the dominant source of such changes. Instead, the bulk of such changes will be prompted by alterations to the individual actor's environment. Of course, the transmission of knowledge regarding these changes "out there" to the mind is of critical significance to the eventual success or failure of any given plan, but plan failure – even on account of inadequate transmission of knowledge – does not present the sort of existential problem for subjectivism that kaledic nihilism's universal plan incoherence does.

Lachmann's approach to the individual is, thus, forcefully against static and equilibrium approaches that trivialize knowledge and change. But, while recognizing that the subjectivist picture of the individual does open the door to the (analytically disastrous) potential for kaledic nihilism, he avoids endorsing it.[9] The key task of social theorists, as Lachmann sees it, is both to resist the temptation to theorize in a way that arbitrarily sanitizes the reality of change and to remain open to whatever forms of order are in evidence.

3 Markets as Adjustment Processes for Reconciling Plans, the Challenge of Plan Adjustment Outside a Market, and the Role of Institutions

Lachmann is committed to theorizing in a way that does not arbitrarily abstract from the reality of change and that focuses on the different forms of order that we witness in the world. This is clear in his discussions of markets as systems for dealing with the unavoidable inconsistency of actors' plans.[10] Only in a world very different and much less complex than our own, Lachmann argued, could we expect plans of complete mutual coherence. In our world, however, we should expect there to be both bears and bulls, both actors who think existing prices are too high and those who think they are too low, both actors who are pessimistic and those who are optimistic. Moreover, in our world, we should expect there to be actors from different cultures, religions, and backgrounds, who disagree on the appropriateness and desirability of certain types of interactions.

As such, for Lachmann, making sense of interpersonal adjustment was of prime theoretical interest. He was, thus, principally concerned with both (1) how the market process works (i.e., the dynamics of plan interaction within the market context which generate its many regularities, including its "equilibrating" forces) as well as (2) understanding the relationship of the market process to the overall picture of social organization. "Inconsistency of plans," Lachmann (1977: 154) explains, is the far more interesting situation, as "[i]n this case we have to argue from the divergence of plans to their disappointment and hence to their revision."

Like Mises and Hayek, Lachmann believed that society was fundamentally dependent on the possibility of plan adjustment and reconciliation, and that plan coordination depends on prices generated within a market process.[11] The subjectivist position, in Lachmann's view, understood more clearly than their opponents that the social function of the price system – the "marvel of the market" – stems not

---

[9] See Lewis (2011) for an account of how Lachmann might have avoided the charges of nihilism that was sometimes leveled against his approach if he had focused more on ontological concerns.

[10] Although we do not spend a great deal of time here discussing Lachmann's view that equilibrium is unlikely, his belief that actors' plans were unavoidably inconsistent is why he does not place much stock in equilibrium but nonetheless offered reasons to understand the market system as an equilibrating system (see Lewin 1994).

[11] As Lavoie (2016 [1985]) would later explore, from the interwar debates it became evident that this represents in some way a distinctly subjectivist insight into the market process. See also Boettke and Piano (2018), exploring how this is reflected in Lachmann's capital theory.

from prices per se but from the processes of price formation taking place within a market context. Contra the market socialists, who seemed to believe that "prices" could be set by fiat and still be meaningful signals, market process theorists understood that what knowledge a given price is "standing in" for will depend upon the reasons why that price is, in fact, *the price*. Prices function as knowledge surrogates only insofar as they are a basis for expectations regarding the possible conduct of others and the availability of certain intermediate and final goods. Only prices generated within a market process can perform these functions.[12]

Although Lachmann viewed market process theory as essentially correct, he nonetheless believed that it was incomplete. The subjective nature of interpretation, in Lachmann's view, represented a serious complication for any account of interpersonal plan adjustments. Interpretation represents one of the major activities that subjectivism attributes to the active mind, which is never confronting circumstances and facts *as such* but instead encounters raw experience, which must be interpreted before it can be incorporated into an individual's overall knowledge. In light of the autonomy of the mind, interpretation is never a fully deterministic process, such that two individuals can arrive at divergent conclusions from identical experiences.

The crux of the issue raised for interpersonal plan coordination by the subjectivism of interpretation, as Lachmann calls it, is that it represents another potential source of mutual incompatibility between individual plans. Indeed, like the autonomous "change of mind," the subjectivism of interpretation means that previously mutually coordinated plans can become divergent as a result of purely subjective causal forces. As we might expect given the relationship between the subjectivism of interpretation and the individual mind's fundamental autonomy, the introduction of another significantly destabilizing factor to the context of interpersonal plan coordination seems to push subjectivist theory in the direction of (interpersonal) kaledic nihilism.

Lachmann approached the problem of interpersonal coordination as one which, unlike the coherence of individual's subjective experience, was not amenable to a theoretical "solution" but would always require evaluating what was actually taking place out there in the world of action. "We have to conclude," Lachmann (1971: 47) argues, "that in a world in motion forces reducing the divergence of plans and other forces tending to widen such divergence will both be in operation,

---

[12] See Horwitz (2004) for a discussion of the role of prices as knowledge surrogates. "The current set of market prices," Horwitz (2004: 314) writes, "is 'data' and 'experience' at the disposal of entrepreneurs; they are 'knowledge surrogates.' They do not 'convey' knowledge, if 'convey' means 'pass on to others.' Rather they make knowledge 'socially accessible.' When we 'use' a price, we don't know what others know, rather we simply are able to act as if we knew what others knew. Prices are, in that sense, surrogates for knowledge." See also Thomsen 1992.

and that it is impossible to say which set of forces will prevail in any concrete situation."

Grappling as much as is possible with the full set of problems involved in mutual plan coordination among a vast number of mutually anonymous yet interdependent agents should if anything amplify, rather than attenuate, our perception of the forces that arise via the market process. As Lachmann (2020: 140) points out, "a competitive market process with consistency of plans constitutes a contradiction in terms. If such consistency were ever to be attained the process would come to an end."[13] We can come to appreciate, for instance, that beyond conveying a bewildering quantity of factual information that individuals would otherwise never be able to access, market prices also reflect how those facts have been interpreted by others *inasmuch as they relate to their plans involving the good in question.*

Prices, thus, mitigate (although not eliminate) the additional burdens of the subjectivism of interpretation for the purposes of the carrying out of economic plans. This is both because price formation demands only that the minimal range of interpretations necessary to be brought into mutual consistency for plan coordination to occur, and because individuals need only arrive at a correct assessment of what others will do in response to a change in price in order to form mutually consistent expectations. Since prices reflect the information and assessment of multiple individuals, different individuals are apt to reach divergent conclusions regarding the most significant influences upon any given price. Where these different interpretations are compatible with the same initial course of action, or where their new knowledge has no immediate consequences for an individual's plan, they have no immediate impact upon price formation.[14] Unless these divergences present a new arbitrage opportunity, there is no reason to think market processes will render them mutually consistent again. On the one hand this highlights the epistemic virtues of the market, as the process of economic coordination is compatible with the presence of a wide range of mutually divergent interpretations that have no systematic tendency towards reconciliation. On the other hand, given the complex interrelationships among economic plans, divergent interpretations that have not yet manifested themselves in mutually inconsistent plans can nevertheless be plausibly expected to do so eventually.

Of course, the market is but one social space among many and economic plans are hardly unique in requiring individuals consider what others are planning as well. Barring exceptional and extreme situations, the most significant circumstances about the "state of the world" that condition each individual's planned

---

[13] See also Lachmann 1977: 124–125.

[14] A simple but relevant example here would be whether a change in circumstances is permanent or temporary.

course of action will be the behavior of other people. Individual plans in all spheres must, therefore, be conditioned upon relatively accurate expectations regarding the potentially relevant plans of others in order to have the most chance of succeeding. Individuals are, thus, by necessity, historians of their own present moment, confronting the ceaseless flow of new knowledge in need of interpretation to assess its significance to their own plans and those of others. Arriving at and maintaining mutually compatible interpersonal plans of any sort will have to confront this monumental epistemic challenge no matter the context.

This is, of course, not to say that coordination among the plans of individuals is impossible: quite clearly, one major way in which individuals ensure mutual compatibility between plans is action oriented towards the establishment of exactly that. But, while the deliberate production, so to speak, of interpersonal coordination – the act of "planning" – is part of the picture, there are readily identifiable limits to what it can be expected to achieve regarding social coordination in general. The difficulty of arriving at and successfully carrying out a plan increases as the number of individuals involved grows: an organization of sufficient size represents a society unto itself, as it develops increasingly complex relationships among the activities individuals within the organization are carrying out. Finally, while the adoption of a coherent intersubjective plan offers a stable basis for interpersonal expectations among the individuals involved, the planners must still consider and adjust to all of the potentially relevant plans external to the organization.

Lachmann believed that the limitations of individuals' ability to achieve mutual consistency of plans via direct interaction means that the extent to which that consistency is achieved will depend instead upon indirect sources of coordination, that is, features of a given context which tend to make individual plans involve certain regularities when they take those features into account. The precise nature of those features will modify the nature and extent to which mutual consistency (as much as is possible given the open-ended and kaledic world of action) is achieved. The most important sources of indirect coordination, however, given the paramount importance of interpersonal interactions, are those which allow for mutually anonymous individuals to arrive at accurate expectations regarding the conduct of others. This is the type of coordination that prices enable within the market system – allowing any given individual A to adjust their plans not based upon particularized expectations regarding each of B, C, and D's plans, but upon the far more modest expectation that all of B, C, and D's plans are made considering the relevant prices.

For Lachmann, institutions facilitate indirect coordination. Lachmann defines institutions as the general class of phenomena within the intersubjective world that individuals use for this purpose. He describes them (Lachmann 1971: 72) as intersubjective "signposts" from which we are able, indirectly, to form relevant expectations regarding the plans of others upon which to base our own actions. Lachmann is exceptionally clear that this is what institutions *do*. "In a complex society such as our own, in which the success of our plans indirectly depends on the actions of millions of other people," Lachmann (1971: 49) asks "how can our orientation scheme provide us with firm guidance? The answer has to be sought in the existence, nature, and function of institutions." Lachmann points out this is also what institutions *are*. Rather than thinking about institutions as a group with some preexisting and external definition, Lachmann is proposing that what makes something an institution for analytical purposes is that individuals are using it in this manner. The extent to which we observe meaningful interaction is, in a certain high-level sense, explained via reference to the existence of institutions *per se*, while the variation in the patterns of individual interaction can in turn be understood in reference to variations in the characteristics of the institutions themselves.

One way to situate Lachmann's concept of institutions is to view him as being concerned with two analytical levels. First, Lachmannn was concerned with the subjective realm of the individual active mind and its associated plan, and second, he was concerned with the intersubjective social world shaped by the interaction among individual plans. Each involved a distinct challenge that raises the possibility of kaledic nihilism. In the former case because of the mind's own autonomy, in the latter because of the autonomy of other minds. In both cases, however, Lachmann identifies their distinct sources of stability. For the active mind, the structure of action and the differential qualities associated with different sorts of knowledge is the source of stability. For the interpersonal world, institutions give us reason to reject the strongest forms of the kaledic nihilist conclusion.

Our overall picture of Lachmann's work can therefore be summed up as follows. Lachmann's commitment to subjectivism, as we noted in the previous section, provides the best starting point for considering his ideas. By rejecting both static and deterministic approaches to the individual actor as being inconsistent with the (ontological) subjectivist conception of the active mind, Lachmann confronts the problem of change which those alternatives had sidestepped. One of the critical insights of subjectivist theory for Lachmann was the manner in which it could account for the ongoing coherence of the active mind without constructing an unreality of mechanistic action or describing an equally unreal incomprehensible flux. Market prices and institutions, for Lachmann, facilitate plan coordination in an open-ended and kaledic world of action. In the following sections, we highlight the overall continuity in theme within Lachmann's writings as well as the continuity of explanatory structure within Lachmann's economics.

4 The Similarities and Differences between Lachmann and Kirzner on Equilibrium

The relationship between Israel Kirzner and Ludwig Lachmann was an important one. It is likely that if not for Kirzner, Lachmann would have remained in the academic wilderness. Kirzner's invitation, and funding from the Moorman Foundation, led to Lachmann's regular visits to New York University (Kirzner 2000). It is from the perch that Kirzner secured for him at New York University that Lachmann would influence many of the younger Austrian economists.

As two of the foremost members of the same intellectual tradition within the same generation, it is not all surprising to find that Kirzner and Lachmann's views on equilibrium and market coordination are similar in many important respects. Both stress the indispensable role played by equilibrium at the level of the individual in economic analysis. Both, following Hayek, understand interpersonal equilibrium in terms of patterns of mutual expectations. Both agree that economic activity in the world around us is never in general equilibrium. And, as such, both see market activity as a constant process of mutual adjustment. Additionally, both argue that the distinctive qualities of market coordination are unique to the institutional environment of the market itself, neither replicable via alternative systems of economic organization nor generally operative in noneconomic domains of social evolution.

As the propositions given suggest, the subjectivist approach employed by both Kirzner and Lachmann understands equilibrium differently when considering different contexts. The role of equilibrium at the individual level is distinct in another sense altogether from interpersonal equilibrium. Indeed, equilibrium at the individual level is also a way to communicate the (usefully tautological) properties of individual decision-making as understood in subjectivist economic theory. At the same time, both Kirzner and Lachmann stress that individual decision-making is not wholly captured by a framework of constrained maximization within given constraints. Some other element beyond means-ends economizing must be present in order to account for individual's capacity for agency, a role filled by both the entrepreneurial element of individual decision-making as described by Kirzner (1967) and Lachmann's emphasis (1978b) upon the active mind as a source of autonomous change.[15]

---

[15] Arguably, at the level of the praxeological account of individual decision-making, the entrepreneurial element of human action in Kirzner and the Lachmannian "active mind" are two ways of describing the same idea. In fact, with regards to their approaches to economic theory, the two

The treatment of individual equilibrium is an important methodological (and ontological) preliminary to understanding interpersonal coordination, naturally the core task of economics as a social science. Both Kirzner and Lachmann approach economics from a fundamentally Hayekian perspective, and accordingly understand the nature of interpersonal equilibrium in expectational terms, as originally described in Hayek's foundational essay "Economics and Knowledge." There, Hayek (1948: 42) observes that what it means for a situation to be a state of interpersonal equilibrium is that "every person's plan is based on the expectation of just those actions of other people which those other people intend to perform and that all these plans are based on the expectation of the same set of external facts, that under certain conditions nobody will have any reason to change his plans." The importance to economics of such an "admittedly fictitious state," Hayek argues, stems from "the supposed existence of a tendency towards equilibrium .... The only trouble is that we are still pretty much in the dark about (*a*) the *conditions* under which this tendency is supposed to exist and (*b*) the nature of the *process* by which individual knowledge is changed" (1948: 44–45, emphasis original).

It is against this backdrop that we can best understand Kirzner and Lachmann's approaches to the questions of interpersonal equilibrium. Kirzner's key insight is his recognition that there is a distinctive capacity present in human action that distinguishes it from pure economizing within a market context. Kirzner understands this capacity as one of "alertness" on the part of individuals operating in parallel to their economizing activities within their present framework of means-ends relationships and that leads individuals to acquire knowledge about potential modifications to the framework itself. "*At the very same time* as man is routinely calculating the optimal allocation of given resources with respect to given competing ends," Kirzner (1992: 160, emphasis original) argues, "he keeps an entrepreneurial ear cocked for anything that might suggest that the available resources are different from what had been assumed, or that perhaps a different array of goals might be worth striving for." It is this distinctive capacity for alertness that drives the kind of equilibrating process to which Hayek refers and which would be absent in a world populated only by constrained maximization.

To illustrate the significance of alertness for the problems of interpersonal equilibrium, we can consider the paradigmatic case of a single-period, single-good market that is not initially in equilibrium, that is, where individuals have imperfect knowledge of their potentially available exchange opportunities.[16]

---

concepts are doing the exact same work in terms of the methodological justification vis-à-vis neoclassical theory.

[16] The single-period, single-good situation, of course, is both the most straightforward case to explain and, in some sense, is always the relevant case. This is because that beneath whatever circumstances or complications someone feels are important (e.g., intertemporal, capital-

The resulting mistakes made by market participants will fall into one of two categories depending on the direction in which they err. The easier case to identify and correct are those plans which mistakenly expected to engage in transactions no other market participants are willing to accept (i.e., they involve trades to the right of equilibrium in a conventional supply and demand diagram). In these cases, the inability to complete those transactions compels revision of the initial plan (which in this circumstance was revealed to have been impossible). Furthermore, although individuals may not always successfully learn from one (or indeed, repeated) mistakes, in part because this sort of error *is obviously a mistake*, the process by which failures like this might prompt equilibrating adjustments is a fairly intuitive one (to which we can always appeal, if needed, to survivorship considerations as well). In contrast, the other sort of error where market participants fail to complete a mutually beneficial transaction due to their incomplete knowledge of market conditions provides none of these obvious indications that something has gone wrong. If market participants are exclusively economizing within given means-ends frameworks, any mistakes of this type will simply persist indefinitely, neither potential counterparty's expectations being disappointed by failing to complete a transaction they do not recognize is possible or erroneously believe would not be mutually beneficial.

Introducing entrepreneurial alertness provides an account of why, in the absence of a mutually incompatible configuration of plans, individuals might come to see the initial pattern as mistaken in some way. Equally important to understanding the tendency towards error correction, Kirzner argues, is that this noticing is taking place within a particular institutional setting, that of the market. Within the market context, discovery of an exchange that would have already taken place but for the imperfect information of the relevant market participants concerning their available opportunities is also discovery of a profit opportunity, and in realizing those arbitrage profits the entrepreneur brings about precisely the state of affairs which would have been adopted in circum-stances of more accurate initial knowledge of market conditions.[17] "The market

---

theoretic, property rights, culture, etc.), there remains essentially a situation of pure entrepre-neurial profit that is always simply arbitrage, when viewed from a suitable theoretical perspec-tive. See, however, Storr and John (2011) for a discussion of why focusing on this single-period, single-good situation may obscure the importance of culture in directing an entrepreneur's alertness.

[17] Individuals as entrepreneurs (distinct from entrepreneur as a catallactic function) are of course as prone to errors and imperfections of knowledge as in other circumstances, but the possibility of error is just one more factor contributing to the continual replenishment of extant opportunities for entrepreneurial profit and does not change, for Kirzner, the essentially equilibrating nature of entrepreneurial arbitrage. Put another way, errors made in pursuit of pure entrepreneurial profit, like all other disequilibrium situations, represent within a market context potentially profitable opportunities. But, what Kirzner means for entrepreneurship to be fundamentally equilibrating is

process," Kirzner (1992: 5) explains, "is understood to provide a systemic set of forces, set in motion by entrepreneurial alertness, which tend to reduce the extent of mutual ignorance." Individuals remain entrepreneurial, alert human actors outside the market context, but the institutional features specific to economic choices within markets are necessary conditions for the presence of a systemic equilibrating tendency for errors of the second sort discussed earlier to be discovered and addressed (cf. Kirzner 1992: ch. 10).

Turning to Lachmann's perspective on interpersonal coordination and the market, we can first note his agreement with Kirzner's substantive propositions regarding the entrepreneurial market process. As Lachmann (1977: 60–61) summarizes, "every state of disequilibrium presents possibilities for profitable activity – be it income, capital gains, or even only the avoidance of losses. Each disequilibrium stimulates alert minds, but by no means all minds, to profitable action, and this action will reduce the chances for further profit." This tendency, however, must clearly only be one (and, given the market process is continually in operation, not a dominant one) among many factors that are simultaneously shaping the course of market adjustments. Accordingly, Lachmann (2020: 3) cautions against the temptation "to ignore such phenomena causing the diversity of market processes, where they matter, for the sake of obtaining a level of abstraction permitting us to speak of *the market process*."

The questions to which Lachmann's writings on market coordination are addressed, however, are somewhat broader than the systematic exposition of why the entrepreneurial market process exhibits a tendency towards equilibrating adjustments even in the absence of plan failures. Arguably, many of Lachmann's most interesting observations regarding the processes of market coordination concern the particular significance associated with certain markets of special interest in the understanding of the economic system (most obviously in reference to capital and asset markets).[18]

There is, of course, a fairly significant difference of perspective between Kirzner and Lachmann when it comes to their attitude towards the importance of equilibrium as a concept for economic analysis. The gulf between Kirzner's conception of market process theory as an expression of a middle-ground position between arid neoclassical formalism and kaledic nihilism and Lachmann's exhortations to radicalize subjectivism and tear down the moribund ramparts of general equilibrium is quite substantial regarding questions of

---

that successful acquisition of pure profit is synonymous with the elimination of the particular gap in the market's overall coordination of knowledge that gave rise to it, and that seems like it does not have much to do with entrepreneurial error.

[18] See, for instance, Lachmann's (1994: 202) discussion of the role of expectations in futures markets.

effective persuasion, rhetorical technique, and coalitional politics. What propositions about the relationship between equilibrium and real-world economic activity, if any, are at stake is less clear. Kirzner (1992: 43) when presenting the different approaches to the market process employed in his work and Lachmann's alternative, describes the central point of departure between their two approaches as the question of the appropriate *terminology* to employ when describing a phenomenon about which (modulus the name) they agree nearly completely.

5 The Self-Similar Structure of Social Systems, the Notion of Orientation, the Centrality of the Plan, and the Theory of Institutions (Again)

The primary way in which Lachmann theorizes is via the consideration of concepts and relations. This is approach emerges from his (ontological) subjectivism and is an additional source for the systematic quality of how he understands the social world. The inapplicability of determinism to active minds and to the intersubjective world that results from the interactions of active minds makes the task of the social scientist, Lachmann (2020: 34) believes, primarily one concerned with providing useful frames of reference. These "ideal-typical conceptual schemes" can assist us in our intellectual task of making events "intelligible by means of causal imputation."[19]

The basic structure with which (methodological) subjectivism is concerned with is the plan.[20] According to Lachmann (1971: 29), the plan "constitutes the natural center of the method of interpretation [i.e., methodological subjectivism] and . . . most of the other concepts we need in order to give an account of human action and its results can be derived from [the plan]." We will, accordingly, use plan analysis as our covering term for the overall conceptual-relational structure Lachmann develops.

The study of plans as isolated entities in themselves is the Pure Logic of Choice, which, as noted, is indispensable but insufficient on its own. "Precisely by virtue of the logical necessity inherent in [the Pure Logic of Choice]," Lachmann (2020: 31) remarked, it "is impotent to engender empirical generalizations. Its truth is purely abstract and formal truth." Additionally, in order to understand plans as components of the active mind, we need to understand

---

[19] As Lachmann (1977: 171) points out, the absence of determinism does not rule out "'negative prediction,' based on inconsistency" and indeed suggests (Lachmann 1977: 178) that "[t]he chief task of the analytical social scientist is to tell the historian what factors will *not* bear a causal imputation."

[20] As Lewin (1994) explains, "Lachmann's economics, with its analysis of the relationships between knowledge, expectations and capital, revolves crucially around the notion of the 'plan.' Economic agents exist in and through time, planning and replanning their actions."

something of the surroundings from which the particular content that comprises those plans comes. Lachmann understands the relationship between knowledge and the plan via a conceptual division between two formally distinct processes of the active mind that enter into planning, that is, an interpretive "taking orientation" and the teleological "deciding" upon a course of action.

Understanding individual plans, accordingly, means describing two component objects. One object Lachmann (1971: 38) refers to is the common-sense notion of "plan," the ordered "directives for action in space and time." The other object is the constellation of relevant knowledge to which the first is oriented or the "orientation map" reflecting the interpretive transformation of "surrounding facts" into, as Lachmann (1971: 38) puts it, a "comprehensive account of means, ends, and obstacles to which a course of action is oriented." This orientation map is comprised of many "points of orientation" (or, equivalently nodal points).[21] Neither of these components by themselves can be truly seen as a (complete) plan. A plan without an orientation map is only a sequence of meaningless directives. An orientation map alone is causally inert.

Lachmann adapts the plain-language notion of orientation (the verb) to serve within plan analysis as a wider term covering the overall psychological processes by which the relationships among the knowledge in a given mind's possession are formed. This psychologically indefinite notion serves, syntactically, as a relational operator between objects and their causal influences. Individual action is oriented to a plan, and plans are oriented by their orientation maps, whose contents are oriented towards the circumstances in which the individual is surrounded. The importance of "orientation" having a technical usage is twofold for Lachmann. First, it collects similar relationships among concepts under a single term where otherwise the similarity might not have been obvious. Additionally, it provides an alternative term to use for social scientific purposes instead of the natural scientific language of "determination." The open-endedness of the world, Lachmann (1971: 38–38) suggests "requires a more flexible form of thought, an 'open' analytical framework which will nevertheless permit us to ascertain the boundaries of action. Orientation is the pivotal concept within this framework."

"The plan" which is the basis for an individual's observed action is at once both a multiplicity of plans at varying levels of abstraction going on simultaneously and a singular entity that encompasses them as what Lachmann (1977: 34) calls a "comprehensive framework." The significance of any particular point of orientation may well shift as one moves between various plans, as is

---

[21] See also Lachmann (1977: 47) and, for the same idea expressed as nodal points, Lachmann (1978a: 58).

most notable when considering the relationship of means and ends. Indeed, most of the means contemplated by high-level plans oriented by relatively abstract ends are themselves the ends of a subplan involving more concrete means, and so on.

There are, additionally, those properties of "whole plans" which have to do with the relationship between the subcomponents and the plan-as-a-whole – complementarity between components on the same analytical level and coherence of the totality. Beyond the mere presence of complementarity, we can also make some assessment of its degree of strength or weakness, how tightly joined a component is to the other components. The entire plan, for instance, may hinge upon a single act or assumption. The same is true for coherence. In fact, the process of making a coherent plan we might describe as bringing about a complementary relationship among its subcomponents. As Lachmann (1977: 200) points out, this works reciprocally: "factors are complements insofar as they fit into a production plan and participate in a productive process." We can also assess the multiplicity of plans across individuals rather than within an individual, that is, the nature of the structure of plans, rather than the structured nature of each plan.

Since the plans of others are part of the circumstances of action to which each individual's plans are necessarily oriented, we are often concerned with a complementarity between the expected actions of others and an individual's plans. We can also characterize plans by the correspondence between the envisioned circumstances to which the internal relations of the plan are oriented and those it will ultimately confront. Moreover, we can assess the extent to which coherence – general mutual complementarity – is present in the structure as a whole. Of course, we should not expect to find complete coherence of any degree at all among all interpersonal plans. Indeed, the structure of interpersonal plans is the most important demonstration that the coherence of each subcomponent does not imply the presence of a coherent plan-as-a-whole, but neither does the absence of such coherence rule out the existence of local complementarities among subcomponents.

The inherent uncertainty of the future makes the inclusion of contingencies an important aspect of individual plans. For instance, like responses to the opening moves of a chess game, the directives for action themselves could include predetermined responses in the event of possible world-states. In a closed system, it is at least imaginable that every potential state of the system could be given an associated response such that a single plan addressed all *possible* contingencies. In an open-ended world, however, this approach cannot hope to cover the entire scope of potential futures, and so other devices are needed as well. Individuals might, for instance, build in triggers with prespecified responses for only certain likely or highly problematic events. Of course, some events matter precisely because the plan was not oriented to their potential occurrence as a significant contingency at the initial moment of decision. Individuals will, when confronted by circumstances outside those where a response is already specified need to adjust on-the-fly and to make use of substitutes.

The stronger the complementarities become between the subcomponents of any given plan, the more potentially disruptive these unexpected modifications to any single point will be for the plan's operation as a whole. Individuals, therefore, face an unavoidable tradeoff between the degree of a plan's coherence and the plan's flexibility to adjust without failure to unanticipated circumstances. We can, thus, imagine plans which are too coherent (i.e., the required degree of dependence among their elements is so extreme as to render them unachievable) as well as potentially which are too flexible (i.e., missing sufficient specificity to secure a relationship between the stated means and supposed ends).

Importantly, failure is always an option, regardless of how coherent (or how flexible) a plan is at the outset. The sequence of actions a plan dictated might be impossible to undertake in the right order in their entirety or not result in the end towards which it was intended. Failure is of analytical significance because of the *reasons* why it might take place, and what we can infer regarding the planner's orientation maps, because as Lachmann (1971: 44) notes, "failure of a plan must be due to inadequate knowledge of the circumstances in which action has to be taken." Depending upon the sort of failure, we can thus gain insight into some of the knowledge from which the plan had been (or not been) oriented to.

In a world of imperfect knowledge, plans are likely to be oriented to at least some information that is inaccurate, either at the moment the plan is embarked upon or when the future does not proceed as expected. The more volatility inherent to various sorts of knowledge, the more likely it is that our expectations might ultimately prove inaccurate and endanger the success of a plan. In our common experience, of course, we recognize this by, among other things, adjusting how our plans navigate between coherence and flexibility. We might specify "rain-or-shine" regarding an invitation to an outdoor event but feel no need for a similar stipulation regarding "gravity or no gravity." When things turn out in an unexpected fashion nevertheless, plans must be revised or abandoned. As Lachmann (1971: 46) says, "unsuccessful planning thus prompts the need for more, and possibly better, planning." Plans do not, however, merely confront the circumstances of their environment. They are also the mental precursor which orients the actions individuals take to shape that environment to achieve their purposes. Lachmann (1971: 48) refers to these plans that modify the intersubject-ive world in a durable fashion as "open-ended."

With open-endedness, we begin to pass from Lachmann's discussion of the preliminary structure concerning the plan itself towards his observations about the elements of the intersubjective world. For Lachmann, the most important of these elements, as we have seen, are institutions. Institutions are, according to Lachmann (1971: 50), "orientation schemes of the second order, to which planners orientate their plans as actors orientate their actions to a plan."[22]

The formation processes of undesigned institutions can be understood much like those leading to other undesigned phenomena. In the case of institutions, this is easiest to see when the institution's existence *is* simply the presence of an ordered configuration of expectations regarding the plans of others. Imagine, for instance, an aspiring musician who, to avoid irritating her parents, goes out to a nearby park on weekend afternoons to practice. This individual's friends, eventually becoming familiar with this habit, begin traveling directly to the park on those days if (as aspiring musicians are wont to do) they are interested in "jamming." A process of further adjustments of other plans to account for their activity (not to mention the intersubjective reality of the gathering itself) leads (potentially) to a gradually increasing number of individual plans oriented towards the intersubjective expectation that, in a particular park on weekend afternoons, there will be a group of individuals interested in playing music with any musicians who are present. Lachmann (1971: 68) describes this process as one in which "successful plans thus gradually crystallize into institutions." This subjective assessment of "success" is crucial in prompting individuals to continue to orient their action on the basis of a proto-institution or to adopt it via imitation of what they perceive was success on the part of others, and thereby lead it to gain greater insulation from the continuously operative process of plan revisions. Note that in some sense it is not really the entire plan which has "crystallized" into an institution, but one (open-ended) aspect of it. Indeed, institutions allow individ-uals to relax the need to confront the plans of others as totalities and instead orient themselves only to the point of significance interaction between them.

Another important aspect of institutions is their multiple significance or, more technically, their "orientational heterogeneity." As a consequence of the open-ended nature of institutions and the subjectivism of interpretation of

---

[22] We might perhaps think to simply translate upwards all of the properties we just considered regarding plans and have a suitable picture of institutions. This move, however, might immedi-ately run into complications. As we noted when considering their importance as the basis for interpersonal plan adjustment among mutually anonymous individuals, institutions are points of orientation regarding a specific sort of significant circumstance (i.e., the plans of others). This is, in fact, what distinguishes institutions from the rest of the phenomena that make up the intersubjective world.

individuals, the significance of an institution as a mutual point of orientation need not (and will not) be the same among those whose plans are oriented to it. Lachmann (1994: 275) suggests that "we might say that an institution is a network of constantly renewable meaningful relations between persons and groups of persons who may not all ascribe the same meaning to the same set of relations." Meeting up for a jam session serves multiple purposes to multiple participants – for example, a way to get out of the house, a social gathering, an opportunity for stylistic experimentation, a gesture of political protest or a pretextual effort at establishing plausible deniability. It is also likely some combination of meanings to each individual attendee. Still other individuals' plans will be oriented towards the existence of the institution but not part of the institution's constitutive structure. Avid bird watchers, for instance, might begin to avoid visiting the park on the days when the jam session is occurring. This suggests at least one initial classificatory scheme for these different orientations, between those "internal" and "external" to the institution itself.

Parallel heterogeneity of orientation also characterizes designed institutions. Most obviously, the significance of an organization (as an institution) will (by design) be different between members, staff, executive officials, clients, donors, regulatory authorities, and so on. Once a designed institution is no longer an imagined result of a plan but is present in open-ended being, other individuals are likely to attach altogether different meanings to it.[23] With designed institutions there is also a tradeoff between the institution's degree of coherence and its flexibility at the institutional level. While that fundamental tradeoff results from the increasing vulnerability of strongly complementary plans in the face of imperfect knowledge, at the institutional level this concerns the specificity of orientation. Increasing the specificity of the orientations the institution is designed to provide makes the expectations formed as a result of being oriented towards that institution more precise (and so therefore able to sustain more strongly complementary plans) but equally decreases the set of plans whose activities can be meaningfully oriented by that institution at all. Further, the stronger are the contemplated complementarities among those heterogeneous orientations from the institution, the greater the likelihood that subtle variations

---

[23] Note that explicitly constituted organizations are at most a proper subset of designed institutions, and that one can find both designed and undesigned institutions superimposed upon each other in any particular situation. There are, it should be recognized, designed institutions which transcend any individual organization (either in function or in time, or both), as is evident in the sphere of designed legal institutions: legislation drafted by a special committee, when passed, will continue to orient action long after that committee is dissolved, while any constitutionally derived system of polycentric governance is by definition larger in scope than any single organization within the system. The convention out of which emerged the United States Constitution is thus one historical example of an organization that designed an institution of greater functional and temporal scope than the organization that designed it.

among those orientations resulting from the subjectivism of interpretation lead to substantive changes to the operation of that institution, with the associated disruption of plans.

Lachmann's view of institutions (especially of undesigned institutions) has much in common with other familiar descriptions of decentralized social processes like Menger's "organic institutions" or Hayek's spontaneous orders. One good way to envision the relationship between Lachmann's undesigned institutions, organic institutions or spontaneous orders is as a Venn diagram in which the two circles are very nearly overlapping but with just enough remaining separation on the sides for two small but clear slivers. In the middle is the obvious overlap where the vast majority of institutions the formation of which we understand, or can observe, are emergent outcomes of decentralized, voluntary choices crystallizing, in Lachmann's terminology, into a set of intersubjective mutual expectations. Given the outsized role played by other individuals in being able to carry out even our simplest plans, a "successful" process of spontaneous order is one which generated, for the relevant individuals, a new undesigned institution in practically every situation. The small but real edges in which a social phenomenon is one of the two categories but not the other are, fittingly, edge cases or situations in which equally small but real variations in what classifies something as spontaneous order. As such, this is a group more or less defined by being plan analysis' version of complex legal hypotheticals or perhaps trolley problems, so we can provide only a few quick examples. The first is provided by none other than Lachmann (1971: 80) himself when providing his outline of the basic concept of liberal political order as a relatively fixed outer shell of designed institutions basic to social order within which the remaining, undesigned institutions are allowed to gradually emerge and develop, including the surprising categorization of both trade unions and firms as "undesigned." Here, the best resolution is to understand the relevant question of design versus undesigned is from the perspective of those charged with organization of the basic outer walls, for whom subsequent designed but not fundamental institutions will be undesigned. Another potential case might be perverse emergent orders, that is, decentralized social processes whose resulting pattern of interpersonal behavior was particularly bad or perhaps worse than would have been the case absent those social practices (see Martin and Storr 2008). In some exceptional cases it might be accurate to describe them as having provided nothing even proto-institutional as it was ongoing from which individuals could take orientation, but this might be a mere conceptual possibility.

The role that institutions play in the overall intelligibility of the social world, and the possibility of complex social order that they make possible, make them an indispensable focus for (methodological) subjectivism. Institutions are a substantive concern because their existence in general is effectively a precondition to acting in a kaledic world and also their presence shapes action in a kaledic world. Of course, once we follow Lachmann in recognizing that the essential characteristic of an institution is that it represents intersubjective signs, it is almost trite to note that the content of these signs and what that content is understood *to mean* by various individuals are also important. In other words, it is not just that it matters that there are institutions, it is also the case that *institutions matter*. All action is both institutionally relevant and institutionally conditioned.[24]

6 On Capital Goods as Institutions

One corollary of Lachmann's notions of open-endedness and his definition of institutions is that capital goods are institutions. This is reinforced by considering the extent to which the significant analytical properties Lachmann discusses regarding capital are those significant to the analysis of any institution and substructure of relationships between institutions.

The "fundamental facts" regarding capital goods that begin Lachmann's (1978a: 2) treatment of capital have familiar counterparts from Lachmann's concepts of plans and institutions. Multiple specificity, as we have seen, is one implication of open-endedness.[25] Capital goods, like institutions, are defined by a particular functional role. To *be* a capital good is to serve as a particular kind of component of a production plan. Importantly, this ties capital goods much more closely than institutions as a whole to notions of individual equilibrium and valuation. While individuals are oriented by institutions in their selection and appraisal of their "best" plan, there is always at least one individual (the owner) for whom this orientation is to the capital good as *means*. Therefore, as Lachmann (1978a: 3) notes, "each capital good is, at every moment, devoted to what in the circumstances appears to its owner to be its 'best' i.e. its most profitable use." Since being a component in a plan is what defines capital goods, it is also not too surprising to find that one of the properties which is intelligible regarding subcomponents of plans in general – complementarity – plays a particularly prominent role among the characteristics of capital goods.[26]

---

[24] In the sense of Weber's (1949) relational triptych distinguishing between a primary class of phenomena (in the case of that essay, economic), those which are causally relevant (but not of primary interest), and those which are conditioned upon the primary class.

[25] Intersubjective persistence is of course closely related to capital goods being durable goods, as well.

[26] Lachmann (1978a: 4) defines capital itself as the "(heterogeneous) stock of material resources," but also recognizes that their materiality is immaterial to their status as capital for the same reason that the divisions between categories like land, raw materials, and capital goods are arbitrary: "the question which matters is not which resources are man-made but which are man-

The relational structure among various capital goods mirrors within its domain the overall relation of institutions and institutional order for Lachmann (1978a: 4) in that "the stock of capital does not present a picture of chaos; its arrangement is not arbitrary ..." yet it is never fully coherent. As Lachmann (1978a: 7) remarked, there always remain "possibilities left open by the existing capital order." Capital appears to be an *almost* self-similar institutional subdomain within the institutional order. Indeed, Lachmann's (1978a: 7) "conception of capital is that of a complex structure which is *functionally differentiated*," about which "the allocation of these functions, and the changes which its mode undergoes in a world of change, is one of our main problems." That said, functional differentiation is not exactly the same as functional specialization. Moreover, change in the capital structure is not quite like changes in the institutional structure.[27]

How different indeed is the structure of capital goods from all other institutions, where change in concerned. In the institutional structure as a whole, as we have noted, there are no systematic influences towards overall coherence. Lachmann, however, points out that regarding capital goods there are several forces that push towards coherence. Capital goods are subject to the basic demand of economic survival. Although Lachmann (1978a: 7) describes the bare existence of this criterion as a "perhaps rather trite" explanation for a systematic tendency towards coherence in revisions to the structure of capital goods, certainly production plans that are not economically viable will be abandoned. But the survival of capital goods does not really rest upon the nontermination of the production plans in which they currently reside. Instead, it is a matter of the economic viability of all those production plans that economic agents believe that the capital good in question is capable of participating in. Upon the termination of any existing plan, after all, its associated capital goods can become capital within a new production plan that (in contrast to the previous one) is at least not demonstrably incompatible with the

---

used. Historical origin is no concern of ours. Our interest lies in the uses to which a resource is put." So Lachmann has already "pointed beyond himself" towards subsequent developments in (methodological and ontological) subjectivist capital theory and the identification of capital as "embodied knowledge."

[27] The problem specific to capital goods being functional differentiation rather than functional specialization reflecting that the functional specificity of capital goods as institutions is already present (at the overall institutional level) from their existence as capital goods. We can consider a similar duality with respect to other parts of the fractal parallelisms, among which multiple specificity provides one further example. The multiply specific nature of capital goods as institutions is an open-endedness with respect to their intersubjective significances: they are available points of orientation for meanings besides those of a capital good (waste byproduct, scrap, consumption good, ill-gotten gains, legitimate military target, etc.). The multiple specificity of capital goods as capital goods is an open-endedness regarding the plans in which they are capable of taking on the significances of a capital good.

current economic system. Alternatively, if no production plan is found in which the capital good can become a part of it will then cease to function as a capital good at all (until this changes).

The operation of market forces, as Lachmann (1978a: 8) writes, "compels the readjustment of production plans which are inconsistent with either consumers' plans or other production plans" and, therefore, "causes the re-integration of the structure by discarding surplus equipment" and generating a tendency towards coherence. Clearly this particular tendency is one which could only occur within the economic context, given the uniquely economic criterion of selection. But, other institutional subdomains, at least those which have internal selection criterion of their own could have analogous processes for correcting identifiable incompatibilities in those institutions when they emerge. For instance, mutually inconsistent judgments are reconciled in superior courts of review via reintegration of some rulings and the discarding of others. Similarly, many systems of political "checks and balances" incorporate some mechanism for unexpected situations requiring adjudication between valid but mutually incompatible institutions within the political system. A good example here would be the ability to initiate a direct recall referendum of mayor or governor. In some respects, these are of course blunt instruments compared to the sort of adjustments regarding capital goods prompted by the market.

The tendency towards coherence in the relationships between existing capital goods is augmented by individual plans oriented by the present structure of capital goods *as institutions* (i.e., as a source of information about the expected plans of others). As Lachmann (1978a: 7) explained, "investment decisions, as to their magnitude, and even more as to the concrete form they are likely to take, depend at each moment on the prevailing composition of the existing capital stock." Lachmann further suggests that it is not just the fact that investment plans are oriented towards the existing capital structure, but that this orientation is substantively one that results in a tendency towards structural coherence. "The shape in which new capital goods make their appearance," Lachmann (1978a: 10) argued, "is determined largely [or oriented] by the existing pattern, in the sense that 'investment opportunities' really mean 'holes in the pattern.'" A related but distinct point concerns the relationship between the "higher-order" nature of capital goods and their role in the mutual coordination of "lower-order" consumption goods. The institutional role of capital is even more evident in Lachmann's (1978a: 58) description here, referring to it as "the *nodal points* of the flows of input . . . and of output."

Thinking about this element of the tendency in the operation of market processes towards a greater coherence in the capital structure we move again towards a view that accords to economic processes a distinct set of characteristics unmatched in other institutions. It is not just that the need to remain in business represents a mechanism of "dispute resolution" among business plans akin to a snap election or a court of appeals. The operation of capital markets also produces a tendency towards complementarity regarding expected future changes in the capital structure in a way those (and other) processes of inter-institutional adjudication do not replicate, and likely can never replicate. One facet of this concerns the properties associated with individual plan revision being oriented by prices which result from market processes. Equally important is the tendency towards an increasing degree of coherence in the structure of market institutions themselves. As Lachmann (1978a: 67) described,

> whenever left sufficiently free from political interference to evolve its responses to such challenges, the market economy has "grown" the institutions necessary to deal with them. In particular, it has evolved institutions to protect the integrating forces of the price system from the disintegrating forces . . .

Elsewhere, he has remarked (Lachmann 1977: 115) that, "in general, the market economy generates the institutions it needs. The lack of an institution may be attributable to the fact that it is not needed." With respect to the institutional order as a whole, however, Lachmann (1971: 135–136) observes the inverse phenomena that "an institution may cease to exercise a function, not because the demand for it has disappeared, but because nobody is capable of supplying it any longer."

This second tendency is, therefore, the fundamental intuition behind Lachmann's view that the forces which prevent a complete coherence among the institutions of the social world as a whole appear to be an irreducible aspect of the interaction among individuals. Within a component of those interactions, however, the processes of adjustment are sufficiently refined that there are not only tendencies towards greater coordination among individual plans, but a tendency for those revisions to make the tendencies themselves stronger via increasingly complementary institutions. This is, of course, largely as a byproduct of competition between adversarial interests.

As we noted in our earlier discussion of the operation of the price system, divergences among subjective interpretations regarding the significance of price movements that do not have immediate consequences for current plans seem to be obvious hazards to future plan coordination. The most important of the institutions that have emerged from within the market system to further refine its operation are those that deal with precisely this issue, namely, futures markets and capital markets. "Price expectations," Lachmann (1978a: 70) observes, "involve intertemporal price relations, and intertemporal price relations cannot be made explicit, hence cannot be adequately expressed, without an intertemporal market." Futures markets, of course, rectify the situation by bringing into existence a price which will reflect those elements of divergent interpretations of the expected future state of affairs. Just as the shared orientation of plans to prices of current goods results in mutually consistent adjustments, so, too, Lachmann (1978a: 67–68) explained, "the economic function of forward markets is to spread knowledge not about what is or has been, but about what people think will be ... in other words, forward markets tend to bring expectations into consistency with each other." Prices relating to particular goods at particular future dates, however, can only exist for a limited range of goods and times. Capital markets and in particular the market prices associated with the expected future returns of various production plans now in being, as in stock exchanges, are, thus, important complements to futures markets.[28]

The stock exchange is also an excellent example as to some of the fundamental reasons why a general coherence within the institutional structure does not (and likely could not) exist. For one, the institutional orientations of the stock exchange (indeed of the capital structure and its surrounding institutions in general) are specifically economic orientations that do not preclude alternative, often incompatible orientations towards those same entities. This is already true when considering the legal framework within which securities exchanges take place. This legal structure, which is complementary to economic institutions insofar as it provides a general orientation towards the existence and legitimacy of the "rule of law," is also replete with friction points where there are contradictory meanings attached to the same entities.

Actions which individuals would expect on the basis of their orientation towards the substance of legal rules may be in tension with those which they would otherwise expect on the basis of their orientation towards economic institutions. Consider, for instance, when successful plans are subject to binding production quotas, or when the imitative revision of a production plan to match that of a more profitable competitor or the takeover of an ineffective firm by

---

[28] Thus, Lachmann (1978a: 69) suggests the central divide between the [methodological] subjectivist understanding of the operation of the economy and the one which animates the view expressed by Keynes in *The General Theory* is their different answers to the following question: "Is the Stock Exchange a suitable instrument for bringing long-term expectations into consistency; is it capable of giving rise to a, socially 'objectified,' *market opinion* to guide investment decisions?" Lachmann concludes we should – with the important recognition that consistent expectations about the future are a *radically* different sort of thing than accurate predictions of it. As he explains (Lachmann 1978a: 71), "the Stock Exchange, by facilitating the exchange of knowledge, tends to make the expectations of large numbers of people consistent with each other, at least more consistent than they would have been otherwise . . . . This, of course, is not to say that the Stock Exchange makes inconsistent capital change impossible: merely, that company directors who ignore the signals of the market do so at their own peril, and that in the long run a market economy substitutes entrepreneurs who can read the signs of the times for those who cannot."

a more successful competitor is precluded by patent or antitrust law. The same orientation towards a general validity of legal institutions concerning property also serves to shelter the open-ended aspects of plans restricting the means by which those potential capital goods can be redirected from their current uses into those that are expected to be more successful. This is not to say such deformation is inevitable, of course, because of the possibility for still further institutions from which individuals take orientation may allow for a stable expectation nonetheless, and so "reconcile" the apparent divergences.[29]

Lachmann identifies economic progress as the result of the gradual "deformation" of the capital structure, over the course of these many alternating phases, towards production plans that have yielded greater economic success. "Both phases," Lachmann (1977: 125–126) notes,

> are necessary and complementary elements of the competition process. Without innovation and product differentiation there would be nothing to imitate, and competition could not exist. Without constant competitive pressure from imitators of successful innovations, innovations would remain a permanent source of monopolistic or oligopolistic income. For economic progress and the function of the market economy, the first phase is as important as the second. How could aircraft, cars, phonographs, and so on of fifty years ago have been developed to their current forms without constant product differentiation?

The cumulative interpretation of these rounds of introduction and diffusion of knowledge is reflected in the contents of today's production plans and the capital goods they employ (as well as many of the absences). Understanding the resultant outcomes as reflecting "progress" even on purely economic grounds is, of course, difficult if other forces shaping the capital structure come to be the dominant ones, such as in the case of wartime industrial mobilization, but here we might perhaps think it is more sensible to view this as a transfer of those capital goods away from economic and towards other purposes.

An overall systematic or structural malinvestment, on the other hand, is the result of a different phenomenon, namely (temporary and ultimately erroneous)

---

[29] Like in the case of the stock exchange's consistency in expectations, we can again here see there is a subtle but important difference between what institutions can and are doing in providing points of orientation as to the expected plans of others and the actual compatibility of those plans themselves. Sometimes an institutional orientation that allows for individuals to "reconcile" two divergent orientations flowing from other institutions will achieve both, but not always. Individuals, for example, can certainly form coherent expectations of this sort via orientation towards the ubiquity of corruption in their environment and thus expect for the legal significance of actions to be of little consequence. This will have consequences for the degree of coherence (and success) that characterizes individual plans, but insofar as it does remove the active tension between otherwise divergent institutional orientations there is no longer a conflict (one "side" has lost).

changes that distort the evaluation of economic success itself. Although we expect malinvestment and the resulting plan failures to be ubiquitous as a consequence of the inherent limitations of individual knowledge in the face of a complex and uncertain environment, we would nonetheless expect mal-investment to result in failed investments that are each failing in their own particular way. As such, the phenomenon which is to be explained when considering systematic instances of malinvestment concerns the presence of identifiable patterns among those failures. As Lachmann (1978a: 100) observed, failed investments resulting from malinvestment must have "enough similarity to make comparison possible," but notes shortly thereafter (Lachmann 1978a: 101) that "in dealing with industrial and financial fluctu-ations eclecticism is the proper attitude to take." The precise factors involved in the generation of any particular episode of systematic malinvestment are certain to change, involving as they do different individuals with different knowledge. Moreover, subsequent episodes will often find it impossible to duplicate the exact malinvestment as was undertaken prior because of the persistence of the open-ended aspects of those plans. Indeed, sometimes the materials of previous settlements are reused in later construction, but equally it is not uncommon to find that later occupants of a site found it preferable to in-fill whatever structures remained and reconstruct the site layout anew.

This is not to say, however, that there is nothing to say, in general, about episodes of systematic malinvestment. The rates of interest that individuals contemplating investment decisions face, for instance, serve as points of orien-tation regarding the threshold of expected degrees of "economic success" that any given investment must be capable of having within the overall pattern of capital goods. Institutional interactions which complicate the task of interpret-ing the rates of interest currently offered to an individual or the functional significance of changes to those rates will, accordingly, make (what later are revealed as) inconsistent decisions more likely. In particular where the substan-tive effect of these interactions leads to rates of interest that are ultimately discovered to be too low to be consistent with the overall patterns of economic interaction, there will accordingly be a class of individuals whose previous plans are now economically unsuccessful.[30]

Lachmann further emphasizes the importance of recognizing that this cannot be a matter merely of there being "too many" or "too few" investment plans in

---

[30] Note that when evaluated purely in terms of this later evaluation of the interpersonal consistency of economic plans, the same sort of mismatches occur for institutional interactions resulting in rates of interest that are substantively "too high" in light of the interpersonal structure of economic plans. These mismatches are no less irreversible than malinvestment, but are generally obscured due to a more limited degree of open-endedness.

general, but that the wrong plans are currently underway. Consequently, an appreciation of the nature of what happened during an episode of systematic malinvestment reveals why actions which are oriented primarily towards a restoration of the pre-crash status quo are likely to be particularly harmful, in that they in effect insist upon the continuation of plans already recognized to be inconsistent and incapable of success.

Additionally, Lachmann notes the reasonable possibility that the owners and managers of ongoing production plans who suddenly find themselves viewed in a new and highly unfavorable light will interpret their own circumstances quite differently. They may well view the current movements as a momentary "panic" and their own plan as more fundamentally consistent with the expected situation once this current crisis resolves. Equally, the fact that it would be more consistent with the interests of individuals in general for components of the current capital employed by that plan to be adapted to other uses does not thereby make it in the interests (even if they agreed this were the case) of the current operators to relinquish them. The capacity for intransigence here depends upon the ability to secure sufficient resources to maintain the existing plan in operation (i.e., resources to support the continued purchase of those complementary components of the production plan not directly owned as well as the retention of the ownership rights regarding the disposition of the relevant capital goods). This often means that the present configuration is entirely dependent on the ability of the present operators to secure investments and loans needed to remain outside of the legal procedures which enforce the "survivorship" constraints of market processes.

Lachmann's capital theory differs in several important respects from the capital theories advanced by Bohm-Bawerk and Hayek. Austrian capital theory as Lachmann understands it in *Capital and Its Structure* and elsewhere retains the distinctively Austrian theme of capital heterogeneity and the associated emphasis upon the importance of the pattern in which capital is employed as more economically meaningful than the aggregate amount of capital deployed. For Lachmann (1978: 12), these properties are fundamentally corollaries of the subjectivist account of the nature of capital goods where to be a capital good is to have a certain defined function within the relationships of overall complementarity that constitute a production plan. This theoretical justification for study of the capital structure instead of the capital stock is where Lachmann is most distinct from the justification offered by Bohm-Bawerk in his original theory. For Bohm-Bawerk, capital heterogeneity and, therefore, the significance of the structure of capital goods are a plausible explanation of a basically classical question. As Lachmann (1994: 197) puts it, Bohm-Bawerk "made use of a certain property of capital resources in order to solve a problem in the theory of distribution, a means to an end." Lachmann's effort to solidify a subjectivist account of the capital structure's analytical importance is hardly unexpected on this point, and it serves the additional function of explaining those areas of Hayek's analysis in *The Pure Theory of Capital* that Lachmann views as still overly informed by a hypothetical situation of long-period general equilibrium. Lachmann, of course, believes reference to general equilibrium is worse than useless as an analytical tool. There is one other point on which we can say Lachmann differs from Bohm-Bawerk, namely that Lachmann views "roundaboutness" (and other single-metric concepts intended to express a unified "state" of a given market's capital development) as ultimately an unworkable concept for its intended purpose.

Contrasting Lachmann's capital theory with Hayek's, there are two points on which their two perspectives differ that are, quite possibly, really two prongs of a single underlying conceptual disagreement. The first of these is not strictly speaking a theoretical disagreement, but their respective major works in capital theory being in one important sense, about different questions. The goal of *Capital and Its Structure*, Lachmann (1978: 12) contrasts with that of Hayek's (1941) *The Pure Theory of Capital* in being concerned not with the "long period ... but in the series of short periods during which resources are shifted from one use to another, and in the repercussions of such shifts." *The Pure Theory of Capital* is aptly named, and even while remaining at a fairly conceptual analytical level, *Capital and Its Structure* does cover more ground related to the way capital recombination is and must be constantly taking place. Lachmann, in a retrospective essay on Hayek's capital theory, is also deeply skeptical (as we may have anticipated) of the continued analytical role of an equilibrium position and "near-equilibrium" comparative statics. "The real difficulty here," from Lachmann's (1994: 196) perspective, "is that of conceiving of any major change, like investment, while the consistency of all places remains unimpaired."

We can conclude our examination of Lachmann's understanding of capital, and of Lachmann's analytical-conceptual apparatus as a whole, by returning to the fundamental reason for the self-similarities among them, their [ontologically] subjective, and intersubjective existence as objects whose significance is understood in terms of the plans oriented towards them. Capital goods and the capital structure are institutions. As such, as Lachmann (2020: 79) concluded, they "have to exist in the minds of agents no less than in reality. In fact, their significance for action derives from the places they occupy in individual plans, that is, from the mental acts by which plans are constituted. Such significance may change, without any change in 'material circumstances,' merely as a result of changing expectations, or changing thoughts."

7 Lachmann's Enduring Influence

In the Introduction, we suggested that Lachmann and the intellectual tradition of (methodological) subjectivism truly traveled together over the course of his lifetime. Arguably, a fruitful way to approach Lachmann's work is to look at it through the lens of his focus on understanding social phenomena as open-ended processes of interaction between active minds. Lachmann provides an account, grounded upon his self-described "radical" understanding of the significance of (ontological) subjectivism, that focuses upon the study of individual plans and processes of interpersonal plan interaction, and the role of institutions as inter-subjective points of orientation in allowing individuals to successfully operate in the necessarily kaledic environment. This kaledic environment is engendered by the (both methodological and ontological) subjectivism of interpretation and expectations of active minds confronting an uncertain, open-ended future.

This focus on the way individuals confront and navigate a future that is not only unknown but unknowable in turn leads to a emphasis upon the central analytical structures of individual plans and the nested and multilayered rela-tionships among them and their components. This also leads to the morpho-logical picture at the intersubjective level of institutions and institutional structure and the properties that those entities and structures exhibit (or fail to exhibit) in light of being subject to perpetual and open-ended change.

In this concluding section, we examine what one of us has described as the "peculiar status"[31] of Lachmann's ideas within his own tradition and in the broader world of (methodological) subjectivist social science. What is peculiar about Lachmann's position in the history of market process theory has nothing to do with the magnitude of his importance to that history and everything to do with the way he is understood to "fit into" it. Lachmann's influence upon "The Salvage of Ideas" (as he once referred to it) within market process theory is, after all, widely recognized – not least in the form of criticism regarding the undue extent of his influence. As is not uncommon concerning "radical" concepts, the other-wise divergent interpretations given to Lachmann between critics and followers agreed that his ideas were a challenge to the extant "mainstream" and even to the orthodox positions within the Austrian school. This is evident in Lavoie's (Lachmann 1994: 1) (approving) description of Lachmann as "a dissident mem-ber of a dissident school." This is also evident in the (accusatory) view of Lachmann's radical (ontological) subjectivism as nihilistic.

The perception of "outsider" status and radical critic is not per se peculiar but is in fact readily intelligible when approached from the perspective of those who originally articulated it. Lachmann most certainly *was* an outsider to the

---

[31] See Storr (2019).

Austrian economic community in New York centered upon Rothbard and Kirzner, and the ideas he brought were quite radical, in some respects. What is peculiar is that this perspective, which originates from the conference at South Royalton and solidified as early as the first years of the Austrian Economics Seminar at New York University in 1975–76, and which was subsequently reified in the course of the vigorous debates among market process theorists in the following two decades on questions fundamental to Lachmann's approach, has by-and-large remained the dominant interpretation a quarter-century later regarding what Lachmann has to offer market process theory *now*. The persistence of this interpretation into the present is peculiar because Lachmann turned out to have been *correct* in some important senses about where the Austrian school was likely to, and arguably needed to, go.

Lachmann, first of all, was correct in understanding subjectivism to be the root cause of market process theory's distinctiveness within economics. He was, therefore, correct in pushing both towards a more thoroughgoing subjectivism as well as greater engagement with other (heterodox) subjectivist strands of economic ideas – most notably G. L. S. Shackle and the subjectivist (in contrast to neo-Ricardian) branch of post-Keynesianism, including (on this margin) James Buchanan. In this, Lachmann was consistently pursuing a path for the school outlined by Hayek. Recall, Hayek (1955: 31) contended that "it is probably no exaggeration to say that every important advance in economic theory during the last hundred years was a further step in the consistent application of subjectivism." And, as Lavoie (1991: 471) suggested,

> It was the arrival at New York University of Ludwig Lachmann, and his challenge that the Austrian school was not radically subjectivist enough, that seems to have provoked the school back onto the road to progress. There is something about this idea of subjectivism that seems to fuel the Austrian theoretical imagination.

Arguably, the major theoretical advances by market process theorists in the last few decades have embraced and built on Lachmann's understanding of radical subjectivism.

Several of the prominent strands of contemporary market process theory are straightforwardly the result of furtherance of this aspect of Lachmann's doctrinal program. The interpretive turn pursued by Don Lavoie (2011) is one such extension of subjectivism explicitly inspired by Lachmann.[32] As Lavoie (1994: 54)

---

[32] See also Prychitko (1994) for a discussion of Lachmann and the interpretive turn where he argues that Lachmann had a flawed understanding of hermeneutics. By this he meant that Lachmann's hermeneutics did not focus enough on the intersubjective or how social circumstances informed the actor's and the analysist's understanding of the plan. According to Prychitko, this is because,

explains, the interpretive turn involved the (re)introduction and (re)emphasis of hermeneutical concerns into market process theory.[33] Specifically, it involved challenging to the notion that market process theory can be an objective science of subjective phenomena and extending the atomistic subjectivism that sometimes plagues market process theorizing to appreciate the intersubjective.

One way to operationalize Lachmann's radical subjectivism and the interpretative turn is to focus on culture and to adopt ethnographic approaches and qualitative empirical methods generally.[34] Arguably, Lachmann's emphasis on subjectivism prompts us to explore what shapes our subjective perceptions and where our meanings come from. Certainly, our meanings come from, or rather are perceived through, our cultures. By culture, following Geertz, they mean shared "patterns of meaning." A cultural system is comprised of a worldview, that is, theories about how the world works, and a value system, that tells us how the world ought to work.

Lavoie has argued that culture shapes entrepreneurship. "The profit opportunities entrepreneurs discover," Lavoie (1991, 36) explains,

> are not a matter of objective observations of quantities, but a matter of perspectival interpretation, a discerning of the intersubjective meaning of a qualitative situation. Profits are not measured; they are "read." Entrepreneurship ... is primarily a cultural process. The seeing of profit opportunities is a matter of cultural interpretation.

Entrepreneurs see the work through their cultural lenses. Culture frames how entrepreneurs see their opportunities and colors how they think of the various paths that they might pursue. Although not the driver of entrepreneurial activity, and not a constraint that blinds entrepreneurs to certain possible avenues, and not a tool that entrepreneurs can use to achieve their entrepreneurial ventures, culture is nonetheless a part of all entrepreneurial action. Following Lachmann, Lavoie argued that it was critical to focus on culture in order to do empirical work that gets at and uncovers the meanings that people attach to their actions and their circumstances.

Chamlee-Wright's work on market women in Accra, Ghana, is a key example of the kind of cultural work that Lachmann's radical subjectivism points towards. As Chamlee-Wright (1997) explains, culture shapes how market women in Ghana make sense of their economic lives, their economic roles and relationships. For example, many market women in Ghana form deep social

---

unlike later hermeneutical Austrians, Lachmann relied more on Dilthey's hermeneutics and less on Gadamer's philosophical hermeneutics.

[33] See Lavoie (2011) for a philosophical and methodological justification of the interpretative turn.

[34] See Chamlee-Wright (2011) for a discussion of operationalizing the interpretative turn.

bonds with even their competitors. As Chamlee-Wright (1997: 137) reports, "most market women, particularly hawkers and mid-level stall traders exhibit a strong sense of camaraderie with the women who trade in their immediate area. The traders form themselves into close-knit groupings, or clusters, sometimes as small as three to five women." Chamlee-Wright also discusses the credit arrangements that they adopt to finance their business ventures. These women rely on rotating credit arrangements known as group *susu* where group members make daily or weekly contributions to a common pool that is distributed to each member of the group in turn. The members of the group who receive an early withdrawal in effect receive a loan from the members of the group with a later draw. The members with a later withdrawal are effectively participating in savings relationship. This arrangement works because members of the group share a cultural perspective, and so have a shared understanding of the nature of their deep connections with one another, of the financial practice, and of the consequences of not meeting their obligations to the group. According to Chamlee-Wright, their cultural frames shape their subjective understandings of this economic and social practice.

Lachmann's radical subjectivism also informs Storr's research on culture and entrepreneurship in the Bahamas (Storr 2004, 2012) and with John (see John and Storr 2013, 2018) on Trinidadian entrepreneurship. According to Storr (2004), there are at least two competing views of entrepreneurship in the Bahamas. One view that we might call spirit of rabbyism, after the hero figure in Bahamian folklore, B′ Rabby, who is a trickster. The other view we might call the spirit of Junkanoo, after the quintessential Bahamian cultural experience, Junkanoo, which is a semi-annual festival that takes a year to prepare for, teaches lessons about the value of hard work, and celebrates creativity and ingenuity. The spirit of rabbyism maintains that entrepreneurship is about the discovery and exploitation of profiteering opportunities, about getting ahead through cunning rather than creativity. The spirit of Junkanoo maintains that entrepreneurship is about working hard to succeed despite obstacles, about getting ahead through creativity and not trickery. Additionally, John and Storr (2018) argue that Trinidadian culture explains why opportunity identification seems to be relatively common among all ethnic groups in the country, but why opportunity exploitation seems to be relatively less prevalent among African–Trinidadians. Understanding the postcolonial culture that emerged in Trinidad and Tobago and the nature and importance of business relationships is key to understanding the subjective perceptions and business practices of Trinidadian entrepreneurs and potential entrepreneurs.

Other market process theorists have extended Lachmann's radical subjectivism by further advancing of his discussion of expectations and the plan. Koppl (2002) builds upon the Lachmannian account of expectations by considering the effects of "big players," actors whose plans are so consequential that other individuals are more or less required to form expectations concerning them directly. The behavior of big players (like central banks), however, can be difficult to predict because they have a significant power to influence the market, are not particularly sensitive to profit and loss, and govern the agents following them. As such, the more big players matter for economic outcomes, the less reliable are expectations.

The increasing importance of software, as considered from a capital-theoretic lens by Baetjer (1998, 2000), demonstrates that Lachmann's emphasis upon the subjective over the material aspects of capital goods can be extended yet further, leading to the description given by Lewin and Baetjer (2015) of capital goods as "embodied knowledge of how to accomplish productive purposes."

Similarly, Lachmann's ideas have served as a point of engagement between market process theorist and the social theorizing of critical realism. For Fleetwood (1995), Lachmann's status as one of the few remaining true students of Hayek makes his work a useful supplement to Hayek's own writings in explaining the contours of that approach. Lewis (2008), on the other hand, engages Lachmann's account of institutions directly, proposing that the account of social reality Lachmann ultimately arrives at may be in tension with his (and market process theorists' in general) commitment to methodological individualism.[35] Additionally, Lewis and Runde (2007) raise a fundamental challenge to how Lachmann understands institutions. Lachmann, they remind us, conceptualizes institutions as recurrent patterns of events that individuals rely on to act in a work characterized by radical uncertainty. But, "Lachmann's account of how socio-economic order is possible under conditions of uncertainty," Lewis and Runde (2007: 176) point out, "presupposes the existence of the very recurrent patterns of events that (on his account) are ruled out in an open socio-economic world."[36]

---

[35] See also Gloria (2019), who also looks to Lachmann in service of a critical stance towards market process theorists' methodological individualism.

[36] Lewis and Runde (2007) raise an additional tension with Lachmann's understanding of social institutions. They argue that Lachmann both presupposes and relies on the causal efficacy of institutions in explaining how institutions make acting in an uncertain world possible and explicitly denies the causal efficacy of social institutions (insisting that human choice is the "irreducible final cause). According to Lewis and Runde (2007: 178), "Lachmann once again appears to be caught on the horns of a dilemma. Either he can acknowledge the causal efficacy of social structure, disavowing the commitment to the unadulterated individualism found in his explicit methodological pronouncements, or he can deny that social institutions have the *sui generis* causal power to affect people's plans and actions and thus bring them closer into conformity with one another, thereby undermining his account of the possibility of socio-

Still, Lachmann was presciently concerned with the analysis of institutions. Not only did he find them of analytical significance for the problems of importance to him but he also forecasted that (given their nature) they would increasingly become the dominant phenomena of interest to (methodological) subjectivists almost regardless of the particular topic under study. Furthermore, this is not merely because of their ubiquitous nature (as Lachmann defined them), such that one could squint through a Lachmann-tinted lens and see "institutions" as the focus of almost any analysis of interpersonal interaction. Rather, institutions are broadly agreed to be fundamental objects of study to be understood in order to make sense of social life.[37] Boettke et al. (2008), for example, highlight the crucial role played by the presence (or absence) of at least some mutual complementarity between institutions in shaping the course of social processes such as economic development. Similarly, Storr et al. (2014) argue that it is local entrepreneurs' capacity not only to restore or recreate a community's institutions but also to be, in themselves, institutional points of orientation in the post-disaster context that make them (as a social category) of particular importance to recovery.

Alongside the ubiquity of these sort of conceptual frameworks (and of course often built into or alongside them) there is of course the study of particular (types of) institutions and processes of institutional change. See, for instance, Harris et al. (2020) concerning property rights. Also, Stringham's (2015) examination of the history of stock exchanges and other financial innovations such as online commerce provides illustrations of Lachmann's observation that novel exchange institutions frequently emerge from within market processes themselves (rather than being dependent upon prior adjustment of other areas within the overall institutional order). As Boettke (2014) notes, this research focused upon what Kirzner (2018) refers to as the "outer limits" of the market – that is, the legal, social, and ethical institutions that orient market participants – Kirzner views as properly outside of the explanatory ambit of the market process itself. Following Lachmann's recommendation for an institutional turn among market process theorists, like the continued development of subjectivism, has also been a source of engagement with other approaches, such as the greater connections being made between contemporary market process

---

economic order." They propose a transcendental realist account of institutions as a potential approach for resolving the tensions in Lachmann's account. Although Lewis and Runde raise deep concerns about Lachmann's understanding of social institutions, they arguably do not end up rejecting his account so much as they offer a grammar for speaking about institutions that simply was not available to Lachmann at the time that he was writing.

[37] See Palagashvili et al. (2017) for a more comprehensive discussion of institutional analysis in contemporary market process theory. This is not to claim that this entire literature is, even implicitly, employing Lachmann's conceptual framework.

theory and both the institutional analysis of the Bloomington School and the constitutional political economy of the Virginia School as complementary approaches within "mainline" political economy.[38]

Lachmann's status, with respect to contemporary market process theory being done now, is thus not the bewildering outsider or the doyen of one faction in an ongoing doctrinal dispute over market equilibration and kaledic nihilism. He is, unmistakably, central to market process theory and those disputes reached a resolution. Regarding theory, arguably, both Kirzner and Lachmann's positions were correct. As it concerns practice, however, the "Lachmannians" won. Nor is Lachmann glimpsing the contours of the questions still on the horizon, such that we might consider what market process theory might come to look like as a school of thought were it to journey in a radically subjectivist direction. The school has, arguably, already undertaken such a journey. Austrian economics has become Lachmann's economics.

---

[38] See, for instance, Boettke (2020). Also particularly noteworthy in this regard is Richard Wagner's (2016, 2020) framework of entangled political economy.

References

Baetjer, H. (1998). *Software as Capital: An Economic Perspective on Software Engineering*. Los Alamos, NM: IEEE Computer Society.

Baetjer, H. (2000). "Capital as Embodied Knowledge: Some Implications for the Theory of Economic Growth," *Review of Austrian Economics*, 13(1): 147–174.

Boettke, P. (2014) "Entrepreneurship, and the Entrepreneurial Market Process: Israel M. Kirzner and the Two Levels of Analysis in Spontaneous Order Studies," *Review of Austrian Economics*, 27(3): 233–247.

Boettke, P. (2020). *The Struggle for a Better World*. Arlington, VA: Mercatus Center at George Mason University.

Boettke, P., Coyne, C., and Leeson, P. (2008). "Institutional Stickiness and the New Development Economics," *American Journal of Economics and Sociology*, 67(2): 331–358.

Boettke, P. J. and Piano, E. (2018). "Capital, Calculation, and Coordination," *Research in the History of Economic Thought and Methodology*, 37B: 9–24.

Chamlee-Wright, E. (1997). *The Cultural Foundations of Economic Development: Urban Female Entrepreneurship in Ghana*. London: Routledge.

Chamlee-Wright, E. (2011). "Operationalizing the Interpretive Turn: Deploying Qualitative Methods toward an Economics of Meaning," *Review of Austrian Economics*, 24: 157–170.

Dekker, E. 2016. *The Viennese Students of Civilization: The Meaning and Context of Austrian Economics Reconsidered*. Cambridge: Cambridge University Press.

Eicholz, H. (2017.) "Ludwig M. Lachmann: Last Member of the German Historical School," *Journal of Contextual Economics – Schmollers Jahrbuch*, 137(3): 227–260.

Fleetwood, S. (1995). *Hayek's Political Economy: The Socio-economics of Order*. London: Routledge.

Fritz, R. and Novak, R. (2022). "Order beyond Equilibrium: Ludwig Lachmann's Bridging of Seemingly Irreconcilable Traditions," *History of Political Economy*, 54(4): 719–744.

Geertz, C. (1973). *The Interpretation of Cultures*. New York: Basic Books.

Gloria, S. (2019). "From Methodological Individualism to Complexity: The Case of Ludwig Lachmann," *Review of Political Economy*, 31(2): 216–232.

Harris, C., Cai, M., Murtazashvili, I., and Murtazashvili, J. (2020). *The Origins and Consequences of Property Rights: Austrian, Public Choice, and Institutional Economics Perspectives*. Cambridge: Cambridge University Press.

Hayek, F. A. (1941). *The Pure Theory of Capital*. Chicago, IL: University of Chicago Press.

Hayek, F. A. (1948). *Individualism and Economic Order*. Chicago, IL: University of Chicago Press.

Hayek, F. A. (1955). *The Counter-Revolution of Science*. London: Free Press of Glencoe.

Horwitz, S. (2004). "Monetary Calculation and the Unintended Extended Order: The Misesian Microfoundations of the Hayekian Great Society," *Review of Austrian Economics*, 17: 307–321.

John, A. and Storr, V. H. (2013). "Ethnicity and Self-Employment in Trinidad and Tobago: An Empirical Assessment," *International Journal of Entrepreneurship and Small Business*, 18(2): 173–193.

John, A. and Storr, V. H. (2018). "Kirznerian and Schumpeterian Entrepreneurship in Trinidad and Tobago," *Journal of Enterprising Communities: People and Places in the Global Economy*, 12(5): 582–610.

Kirzner, I. (1967). "Methodological Individualism, Market Equilibrium, and Market Process," *Il Politico*, 32(December): 787–799.

Kirzner, I. (1992). *The Meaning of Market Process: Essays in the Development of Modern Austrian Economics*. New York: Routledge.

Kirzner, I. (2000). *The Driving Force of the Market*. New York: Routledge.

Kirzner, I. (2018). "The Limits of the Market: The Real and the Imagined," in P. Boettke and F. Sautet (eds.), *The Collected Works of Israel M. Kirzner: Reflections on Ethics, Freedom, Welfare Economics, Policy, and the Legacy of Austrian Economics*. Indianapolis, IN: Liberty Fund: 384–394.

Koppl, R. (2002). *Big Players and the Economic Theory of Expectations*. New York: Palgrave Macmillan.

Lachmann, L. (1971). *The Legacy of Max Weber*. Berkeley, CA: The Glendessary Press.

Lachmann, L. (1977). *Capital, Expectations, and the Market Process: Essays on the Theory of the Market Economy*, W. Grinder (ed.). Kansas City, MO: Sheed Andrews and McMeel.

Lachmann, L. (1978a [1956]). *Capital and Its Structure*. Menlo Park, CA: The Institute for Humane Studies.

Lachmann, L. (1978b) "An Austrian Stocktaking: Some Unanswered Questions and Tentative Answers," in L. Spadaro (ed.), *New Directions in Austrian Economics*. Kansas City, MO: Sheed Andrews and McMeel: 1–18.

Lachmann, L. (1994). *Expectations and the Meaning of Institutions*, D. Lavoie (ed.). New York: Routledge.

Lachmann, L. (2020 [1986]). *The Market as an Economic Process*. Arlington, VA: Mercatus Center at George Mason University.

Lavoie, D. (1991). "The Progress of Subjectivism," in N. de Marchi and M. Blaug (eds.), *Appraising Economic Theories: Studies in the Methodology of Research Programs*. Aldershot: Edward Elgar: 470–491.

Lavoie, D. (2011). "The Interpretive Dimension of Economics: Science, Hermeneutics, and Praxeology," *Review of Austrian Economics*, 24: 91–128.

Lavoie, D. (2016 [1985]). *Rivalry and Central Planning*. Arlington, VA: Mercatus Center at George Mason University.

Lavoie, D. and Chamlee-Wright, E. (2000). *Culture and Enterprise: The Development, Representation, and Morality of Business*. New York: Routledge.

Lewin, P. (1994) "Knowledge, Expectations, and Capital: The Economics of Ludwig M. Lachmann," *Advances in Austrian Economics*, 1: 233–256.

Lewin, P. (2018). "Ludwig Lachmann: Enigmatic and Controversial Austrian Economist," *Liberty Matters*, July. https://oll.libertyfund.org/page/liberty-matters-peter-lewin-ludwig-lachmann-austrian-economics. Accessed January 1, 2023.

Lewin, P. and Baetjer, H. (2015). "The Capital-Using Economy," in P. Boettke and C. Coyne (eds.), *The Oxford Handbook of Austrian Economics*. Oxford: Oxford University Press: 145–163.

Lewis, P. (2008). "Solving the 'Lachman Problem': Orientation, Individualism, and the Causal Explanation of Socioeconomic Order," *American Journal of Economics and Sociology*, 67(5): 827–857.

Lewis, P. (2011). "Far from a Nihilistic Crowd: The Theoretical Contribution of Radical Subjectivist Austrian Economics," *Review of Austrian Economics*, 24: 185–198.

Lewis, P. and Runde, J. (2007). "Subjectivism, Social Structure and the Possibility of Socio-economic Order: The Case of Ludwig Lachmann," *Journal of Economic Behavior and Organization*, 62(2): 167–186.

Loasby, B. J. (1998). "Ludwig M. Lachmann: Subjectivism in Economics and the Economy," in R. Koppl and G. Mongiovi (eds.), *Subjectivism and Economic Analysis: Essays in Memory of Ludwig M. Lachmann*. New York: Routledge.

Martin, N. P. and Storr, V. H. (2008) "On Perverse Emergent Orders," *Studies in Emergent Order*, 1: 73–91.

Mises, L. (1949). *Human Action*. San Franscico: Fox & Wilkes.

Palagashvili, L., Piano, E., and Skarbek, D. (2017). *The Decline and Rise of Institutions: A Modern Survey of the Austrian Contribution to the Economic Analysis of Institutions.* Cambridge: Cambridge University Press.

Prychitko, D. L. (1994) "Ludwig Lachmann and the Intrepretive Turn in Economics: A Critical Inquiry into the Hermeneutics of the Plan," *Advances in Austrian Economics*, 1: 303–319.

Storr, V. H. (2019). "Ludwig Lachmann's Peculiar Status within Austrian Economics," *The Review of Austrian Economics*, 32(1): 53–75.

Storr, V. H. (2004). *Enterprising Slaves and Master Pirates: Understanding Economic Life in the Bahamas.* New York: Peter Lang.

Storr, V. H. (2012). *Understanding the Culture of Markets.* New York: Routledge.

Storr, V. H., Haeffele, S., and Grube, L. (2014). *Community Revival in the Wake of Disaster: Lessons in Local Entrepreneurship.* New York: Palgrave Macmillan.

Storr, V. H. and John, A. (2011) "The Determinants of Entrepreneurial Alertness and the Characteristics of Successful Entrepreneurs," *Annual Proceedings of the Wealth and Well-Being of Nations*, 3: 87–108.

Storr, V. H. and John, A. (2020). *Cultural Considerations within Austrian Economics.* Cambridge: Cambridge University Press.

Stringham, E. P. (2015). *Private Governance: Creating Order in Economic and Social Life.* Oxford: Oxford University Press.

Thomsen, E. F. (1992). *Prices and Knowledge: A Market Process Perspective.* New York: Routledge.

Vaughn, K. (1994). *Austrian Economics in America: The Migration of a Tradition.* New York: Cambridge University Press.

Wagner, R. E. (2016). *Politics as a Peculiar Business: Insights from a Theory of Entangled Political Economy.* Cheltenham: Edward Elgar.

Wagner, R. E. (2020). "Entangled Political Economy: Mixing Something Old with Something New," *GMU Working Papers in Economics*, 20–33.

Weber, M. (1949). "'Objectivity' in Social Science and Social Policy," in E. A. Shils and H. A. Finch (eds.), *Max Weber on the Methodology of the Social Sciences.* Glencoe, IL: Free Press: 49–112.

Cambridge Elements

Austrian Economics

Peter Boettke
George Mason University
Peter Boettke is a Professor of Economics & Philosophy at George Mason University,
the BB&T Professor for the Study of Capitalism, and the director of the F. A. Hayek Program
for Advanced Study in Philosophy, Politics and Economics at the Mercatus Center
at George Mason University.

About the Series
This series will primarily be focused on contemporary developments in the Austrian
School of Economics and its relevance to the methodological and analytical
debates at the frontier of social science and humanities research, and the continuing
relevance of the Austrian School of Economics for the practical affairs
of public policy throughout the world.

Cambridge Elements ≡

Austrian Economics

Printed in the United States
by Baker & Taylor Publisher Services